UNCONQUERABLE

BORIS STARLING

FOREWORD BY **PRINCE HARRY**

UNCONQUERABLE
THE INVICTUS SPIRIT

FOUNDATION

HarperCollins*Publishers*

HarperCollins*Publishers*
1 London Bridge Street
London SE1 9GF

www.harpercollins.co.uk

First published by HarperCollins*Publishers* 2017

1 3 5 7 9 10 8 6 4 2

© Boris Starling 2017

Boris Starling asserts the moral right
to be identified as the author of this work

Plate-section photographs courtesy of the competitors, with the exception of:
p1 (bottom) Roger Keller and p8 (top) www.LohkemperPhotography.de

While every effort has been made to trace the owners of copyright material
reproduced herein and secure permissions, the publishers would like to
apologise for any omissions and will be pleased to incorporate missing
acknowledgements in any future edition of this book

A catalogue record of this book is
available from the British Library

HB ISBN 978-0-00-824008-0
PB ISBN 978-0-00-819650-9

Printed and bound by
CPI Group (UK) Ltd, Croydon, CR0 4YY

MIX
Paper from
responsible sources
FSC
www.fsc.org   FSC™ C007454

This book is produced from independently certified FSC paper
to ensure responsible forest management

For more information visit: www.harpercollins.co.uk/green

For those who competed in London and Orlando,
for those who are competing in Toronto, and for
those who will compete in Sydney and beyond.
You are an inspiration, each and every one of you.
You are unconquered.

CONTENTS

ABOUT THE INVICTUS GAMES

The Invictus Games are an international multisport event for WIS (wounded, injured and sick) Armed Services personnel and veterans. The Games use the power of sport to inspire recovery, support rehabilitation and increase awareness of the sacrifices made by those who serve.

The first Invictus Games took place in London on 10–14 September 2014. Thirteen nations were represented and 413 competitors took part: Afghanistan, Australia, Canada, Denmark, Estonia, France, Georgia, Germany, Italy, Netherlands, New Zealand, the United Kingdom and the United States. Competitions took place across nine adaptive sports: archery, athletics, indoor rowing, powerlifting, road cycling, sitting volleyball, swimming, wheelchair basketball and wheelchair rugby. The Presenting Partner, Jaguar Land Rover, also offered a driving challenge.

The inaugural Invictus Games have created the blueprint for inspiring many more 'wounded warriors' on their journey of recovery, and the success of the Games prompted the organisers to stage a follow-up. They know that hundreds more wounded warriors around the world could benefit from taking part in the Invictus Games. So they established the Invictus Games Foundation to develop and pursue the Invictus Games legacy and continue to make a difference to the lives of wounded, injured and sick Service personnel around the world.

There was not enough time to get one up and running in 2015, so the second Invictus Games took place in Orlando, Florida, on 8–12 May 2016. All the nations from 2014 participated again, plus Jordan. Wheelchair tennis was added to the roster of sports. Altogether 485 competitors took part.

The third Invictus Games are taking place in Toronto on 23–30 September 2017. Romania and Ukraine are competing for the first time, and golf has been added to the list of sports. More than 550 competitors are taking part.

The fourth Invictus Games will take place in Sydney on 20–27 October 2018.

FOREWORD BY PRINCE HARRY

This book gives an insight into the lives of servicemen and women who have been wounded or faced life-changing illness in the Armed Forces: what goes through their minds at the moment of injury; the effect this event has on their family and friends; the long and often painful road to recovery; where they find the strength and courage to keep fighting; and how they embrace a life that they had never imagined.

The stories of the men and women in this book are some of the most inspiring examples of courage and determination you will read anywhere. Not because they are superhuman; in fact, quite the opposite – they are normal people who have fought hard to overcome seemingly insurmountable challenges and come back stronger! I am extremely grateful to them for sharing their experiences so honestly. I am also delighted that they have been given this opportunity to tell their stories and, in doing so, inspire millions of people around the world by their example.

It is important to remember that this book highlights just a handful of stories from Invictus Games competitors who have experienced life-altering events. There are hundreds of other servicemen and women who showcase their Invictus spirit every day by overcoming injury and illness, reminding us what grit, determination, defiance and the will to succeed really mean.

This book recognises the amazing example set by our servicemen and women, their contribution to society and ultimately the sacrifices they are prepared to make for their country.

We can all draw strength from these breathtaking stories. The men and women who feature in this book, and the many others like them around the world, are a constant reminder that it is possible to overcome adversity, and that the impossible is possible if you have the will.

I am proud that the Invictus Games continue to change lives every day and am confident that you will be as moved and inspired by these stories as I have been.

Prince Harry

INTRODUCTION

When I started *Unconquerable*, my thinking was guided by two lines of belief. First, that the Invictus Games would be like the Olympics or Paralympics, where the medal table is both pride and curse and where lip service is paid to the importance of taking part while all the attention goes to those standing on the podium. Second, that there'd be a definite hierarchy within the WIS network. The wounded, those who'd lost limbs in battle, would, in a perverse way, be the glamour squad, the ones who'd suffered the most and whose very appearance would be a constant reminder of the sacrifices they'd made. Behind them would come the injured, and bringing up the rear would be the sick, because everybody gets sick now and then, don't they?

I could hardly have been more wrong on both counts if I'd tried.

When you watch the Olympics and Paralympics, most of the pleasure you get is from watching people who are the very best in the world at what they do. Their backstories are usually irrelevant, though not always – the impact of, for instance, the German weightlifter Matthias Steiner's gold medal at Beijing in 2008 is magnified severalfold when you know that his wife, Susann, had been killed in a car crash the year before and he'd promised her as she lay dying that he'd become champion in her memory.

Olympians and Paralympians dedicate their lives to those few minutes every four years, and are judged on the order in which they finish. Those who compete in the Invictus Games are very different. Who wins which medal is almost irrelevant. It's not the finish line which counts, it's the start line. Even to get to that start line after what these people have been through is a triumph in itself, a triumph made sweeter by the demands and joys of competition – the camaraderie, the challenge, the banter, the exploration of one's limits.

And because everyone who competes has gone through some version of hell to get there, there is no comparing or grading of afflictions. More than one triple amputee told me that, yes, what they'd been through was horrific and, yes, day-to-day living could be very tricky, but there was also an acceptance of their situation and a determination to make the best of it. Their limbs weren't going to grow back, but nor were they going to deteriorate still further. The worst had come and gone. Crack on.

Compare that to those undergoing prolonged cancer treatment or suffering the excruciating debilitations of post-traumatic stress disorder (PTSD). Less visible ailments, sure, but no less serious for that: in some ways more serious, with the uncertainty of what might happen in the future and the fluctuations in how they feel not just week to week but day to day and sometimes even hour to hour.

I didn't know any of this at the start, but I learned pretty fast. I already knew that watching world-class athletes achieve greatness was inspiring. Now I learned that watching wounded warriors achieve greatness was more than inspiring. It was life-changing.

As a writer, you do some projects for love and some for money. Now and then, though very seldom, you get to work on something which is an absolute privilege. Writing *Unconquerable* was one of those rare, precious things. Every day I felt humbled by the extraordinary stories I was hearing and awestruck at the astonishing resilience of the human spirit.

I hope that when you read this book you see why.

Boris Starling, May 2017

ACKNOWLEDGEMENTS

Thank you to all those without whom this book could not have happened.

Those competitors who gave up their time over coffee, beer, Skype or e-mail to talk to me with such unflinching candour: Amy Baynes, Josh Boggi, Darlene Brown, Bart Couprie, Kai Cziesla, Seb David, Christine Gauthier, Mike Goody, Maurice Manuel, Stephan Moreau, Sarah Rudder, Maurillia Simpson, Fabio Tomasulo, Phil Thompson, Zoe Williams, Mary Wilson and Rahmon Zondervan.

The wonderful Cake Lady, Kath Ryan, for telling me her own unique story.

Sara Trott, for her insight into what life is like for friends and families.

At the Invictus Games Foundation, Dominic Reid, Julie Burley and Mickey Richards.

The staff of the Defence Medical Rehabilitation Centre at Headley Court, particularly Peter Haslam, Lt Col Rhodri Phillip, Kate Sherman, Mark Thoburn and Lt Col Gareth Thomas.

Hannah Lawton of the GB Rowing Team Paralympic Programme and all the other coaches and hopefuls at the Bath University training weekend, who tolerated me asking them questions when they had better things to do.

At HarperCollins, Liz Dawson for suggesting me for this project, Oliver Malcolm for agreeing with her, Emily Arbis for pulling everything together, and Simon Gerratt and Jane Donovan for eagle-eyed copy-editing.

At Caskie Mushens, Juliet Mushens and Nathalie Hallam.

At Kensington Palace, Kat McKeever and of course Prince Harry, whose passion for and eloquence about the Invictus Games cause comes from the heart and is awe-inspiring.

My parents, David and Judy Starling, and my in-laws, Jenie and Jeremy Wyatt.

And as always, my wife, Charlotte, and our children, Florence and Linus, the three captains of my soul.

INVICTUS

Out of the night which covers me,
Black as the pit from pole to pole,
I thank whatever gods may be
For my unconquerable soul.

In the fell clutch of circumstance
I have not winced nor cried aloud.
Under the bludgeoning of chance
My head is bloody, but unbowed.

Beyond this place of wrath and tears
Looms but the horror of the shade,
And yet the menace of the years
Finds, and shall find me, unafraid.

UNCONQUERABLE

It matters not how strait the gate,
How charged with punishments the scroll,
I am the master of my fate:
I am the captain of my soul.

William Ernest Henley, 1875

PROLOGUE

THE NIGHT WHICH COVERS ME

1 March 2008

Five miles above the earth, the night inky-black outside, the young officer bit down hard on his anger.

The transport plane was full of blokes going home: tired, happy, relieved to have survived their tours in Afghanistan pretty much unscathed, at least on the outside. The officer wasn't part of these men: he was a Second Lieutenant in the Household Cavalry and his men were still out in Afghanistan. He was going home not because he wanted to but because he'd been ordered to, and he wasn't at all happy about it. He'd been in Afghanistan for 10 weeks and his tour was supposed to be 14. Ten weeks was easily long enough to get a campaign medal, but he didn't much care about that: he cared about being with his men until the end.

He'd loved it out in Afghanistan. For the first time in his life he'd been treated as a normal bloke rather than anyone special. He'd trained hard and done his job well: patrolling the deserted bombed-out streets of Garmsir, southern Helmand Province, defending his position from Taliban mortar and machine-gun attacks, and calling in airstrikes on enemy positions. To the pilots who dropped 500lb bombs on the co-ordinates he gave them he was just 'Widow Six Seven', his callsign – they didn't know his real name and they wouldn't have cared if they had. It was the people back home who cared, not the men in theatre. He'd slept alongside those men in Hesco wire-mesh gabion bunkers and used the rounded ends of missile cases as shaving bowls with them. He was a good soldier and a good man – that was all that mattered to them.

There was only really one thing the officer hadn't seen, and that was death or serious injury. Sure, he'd called in many medical evacuations for soldiers who'd been blown up by improvised explosive devices (IEDs) or shot in contact with Taliban fighters. Sometimes he'd said 'op vampire' when the casualty needed a lot of blood, and that always sent shivers down his spine. He'd lain in bed late at night and felt the place shaking from the downforce of a Chinook or a Black Hawk carrying the wounded, but he'd never seen someone killed or maimed.

Here, now, on the transport plane high above the Black Sea, he saw it.

The plane had been late leaving Kandahar Airfield because it had to wait for the coffin of a Danish soldier. Morten Krogh Jensen, just 21, had only been in Afghanistan three weeks. He'd been one of those people whom everyone had naturally liked: in a no-holds-barred team review of each soldier's performance, Krogh had been the only one with nothing negative said about him whatsoever. Now his body was being repatriated to the seaside town of Frederikssund, where he'd helped his friends paint the hulls of boats in the harbour, where he'd convened groups to head for techno concerts in nearby Copenhagen, and where his family waited with an unfathomable hole in their lives.

Krogh's coffin was kept out of sight, as were three British soldiers who'd been seriously wounded and were being taken back to Britain's premier military hospital at Selly Oak in Birmingham. These soldiers were behind a curtain at the front of the plane, yet now and then the curtain blew open slightly and the young officer could see them. They were in a bad way: wrapped up in what looked like clingfilm and with bandages round the stumps of missing limbs. One of them was clutching a tiny bottle full of shrapnel removed from his skull. They were all in induced comas.

The young officer saw all this, as raw and visceral a face of war as could be. Too raw and visceral to be shown on the news, too raw and visceral for a public who didn't, couldn't, know the true cost of conflict unless they knew this. He hadn't prepared himself, and the sight shocked and rattled him somewhere deep within himself. It certainly put his own frustrations into perspective.

The transport plane made its relentless way north-west, over the sleeping cities of Europe through which so much history had marched. It was daylight when the plane landed at Birmingham to unload the three wounded men, and mid-morning by the time it made the short hop back to RAF Brize Norton, where most people were disembarking. The young officer was 41st off the plane. No special treatment.

No special treatment, that was, until his feet stepped onto the tarmac. He may have been 41st off the plane, but he was still third in line to the throne, and numbers one and two were waiting for him. In Afghanistan he had been Second Lieutenant Wales. Now he was Prince Harry again.

He'd been pulled out for his own safety after details of his presence in Afghanistan had been made public. Once the news was out it was out, and so too was Harry.

He drove back to Windsor with his father, Prince Charles, and his brother, Prince William. The English countryside rolled past the windows, so much gentler and greener than the harsh browns of Afghanistan.

He thought about the men he'd seen behind that curtain. He wondered what he could do for them. There had to be something. But what? He had questions but no answers; he had a problem with no solution. But at least he was asking those questions. At least he recognised there was a problem.

Neither Prince Harry nor anyone else knew it at the time, but he had sown the first seeds of what would eventually blossom into the Invictus Games.

MAURICE MANUEL, DENMARK

Maurice Manuel speaks perfect English. That in itself isn't unusual for a Dane, but in Maurice's case his fluency comes from more than just education. His father was American – a Vietnam vet who did two tours of duty in that most agonising of wars and then decided to stay in Germany.

'He was told it was a better life there than it would have been for a black army veteran back home at the time.' A conflict which was becoming polarisingly unpopular and with the civil rights movement at its most fractious: whoever gave Manuel Snr that advice was probably spot on. So stay in Germany he did. He became a radiologist and married Maurice's mother, a Danish lady.

The lure of the military burned strongly in Maurice, even though in Denmark soldiers weren't so revered as they are in the United States or respected as much as they are in the United Kingdom. The majority of Danes opposed intervention in both Iraq and Afghanistan right from the start. When Maurice went out to serve in the Middle East, therefore, he knew he was doing so for a country at best ambivalent about his presence there.

Maurice did two tours in Iraq and four in Afghanistan. He was a military policeman for all but the last one, for which he studied

Pashto, the official language of Afghanistan, so he could become a combat interpreter and help liaise between the Western forces and the Afghan National Army.

It was 14 December 2010 when his life changed. He doesn't need to look the date up, he remembers it as easily as he would his own birthday.

'It was a completely normal patrol. We were down there before sunrise, and I was in charge of the sound commander.' A sound commander is, more technically, a 'wide area mass notification system': it can broadcast messages to be heard far away, and the operator can also programme in sound effects such as suppressive gunfire and helicopter rotors to give the impression of a larger military presence than actually existed.

'I left it somewhere while we continued the patrol. When we'd finished, I went to get it. I saw it down the end of a path. I'd not gone 20 metres when I thought: "I don't think this path's been swept [for IEDs]." And that second, that very second, I stepped on one. There was dust everywhere. I was thrown backwards, I looked down, and I saw the bottom of my right fibia sticking out of my boot. I grabbed a tourniquet and wrapped it round my thigh as hard as I could.'

Some of his colleagues were a kilometre and a half away when the IED went off, and even at that distance they heard not just the explosion but Maurice's shout of pain too. Not only did they have to go back and get him, but then take him out another 2km on a stretcher, as the Merlin medevac helicopter wouldn't come in closer than that during a TIC (troops in contact) situation for fear that it too would be a target for attack.

The next seven or eight hours of Maurice's life are just fragmentary memories through a haze of shock, morphine and 'whatever heavier they gave me'. Now and then he woke for a few seconds to see lights in an operating theatre or surgeons leaning over him, the next moment he was out cold again. They kept him in Bastion for three days before flying him home the scenic route – Qatar, Germany, the UK and finally Denmark, where the surgeon told him he'd never be able to run again and he'd have to wear corrective shoes.

'Let's amputate,' Maurice said.

But the surgeon refused. He thought it would be better to keep everything intact if possible. Reluctantly, Maurice agreed, and spent the next nine months in rehab, trying to build the damaged leg back up to some kind of strength again – 'It was a fiasco from the get-go.'

Maurice did his research: he found medical papers online, he talked to a couple of US Rangers who'd sustained similar injuries. Then he went back to the surgeon and told him they'd tried rehab, it hadn't worked, and now he was insisting on what he'd asked for at the start: he wanted to be a below-the-knee amputee. This time the surgeon had little choice but to agree.

'I had the chop on 15 August 2011.' Another date he doesn't need to look up. 'Three weeks later I was up and walking on a prosthetic. Two months after that I was running.'

THE NIGHT WHICH COVERS ME

The invitation to the 2014 Invictus Games came through the Soldier Project at the Danish Handicap Association, and Maurice didn't need asking twice. He'd been a keen sprinter and basketballer before his injury, so he signed up for track and field, wheelchair basketball (where he was made captain and coach) and wheelchair rugby too.

It was a busy schedule for anyone, and made more so by the fact that one of his family members was unwell and he had to spend a lot of time caring for them. If it stressed him, he never let it show. He competed in the best traditions of both soldier and sportsman: no quarter asked nor given on the field of play, but generous in his praise and commiserations once the final whistle had been blown or the finish line crossed.

He won a silver in the javelin and three bronzes, in the 200m Men Ambulant IT1, the wheelchair basketball and the wheelchair rugby. But a greater prize than any of those was waiting. The organising committee saw his contribution on and off the field, saw his determination and integrity, and gave him the Land Rover Unconquerable Soul Award. Out of more than 400 competitors, Maurice had been deemed the one who most embodied the Invictus spirit.

He smiles when I remind him of this. 'It was an honour beyond measure. Words can't express how special that was. It still gives me goosebumps, even thinking about it.' As for Prince Harry, 'I can't tell you how important it is that a person like him does this. He's a prince, sure, but he's an ordinary guy too. Thousands of people are so grateful to him.'

Two years later Maurice was back in Invictus Games action, this time in Orlando, Florida. This time he captained the wheelchair basketball team to victory over the Netherlands in the bronze medal match, and then went one better in wheelchair rugby with silver, losing to the USA in the final – much to the relief of then Vice President Joe Biden, whose pre-match pep talk to the American team had been along the lines of 'I have to meet the Danish Prime Minister next week and I don't want to have to wear an awkward smile'.

Five medals from two Games, then, but no golds. Not that Maurice minds. 'It's been an honour and a privilege to be here,' he said after the wheelchair rugby final in Orlando. 'Words can't describe what it means. This is for physical disabilities and PTSD [post-traumatic stress disorder], it's for proving to the world and ourselves that we can. Every single athlete here has risen to the occasion, there's no doubt about that.'

None more so than Maurice, the Unconquerable Soul himself. He now plays professional wheelchair basketball in Florida for the Fort Lauderdale Sharks while studying for a Bachelor's in Crisis Management at Everglades University. He does more with one leg than most people do with two. 'If you can think it, you can do it,' he says simply.

Before we end the Skype call, I tell him I have one more question. 'Shoot,' he says.

OK. On the ARSSE (Army Rumour Service) website, there's quite a lot of chat from female contributors about how he's so 'easy on the eye' and how they needed 'a lie down after seeing him on the basketball court'. What does he think about being an Invictus Games sex symbol?

He throws back his head in laughter, flashing the whitest pair of teeth I've seen in a long while. 'Get outta here!'

1

FIND ME UNAFRAID

The English market town of Salisbury can be a bleak place on a winter's day. Four o'clock in the afternoon, the market traders are packing away whatever they've failed to sell beneath awnings flapping in the wind, people are hurrying from one place to another, coats zipped up to their necks and hands thrust deep in pockets. It doesn't look like a place with one of the UK's most important cathedrals, let alone somewhere so intimately connected with the world-famous Stonehenge, just up the road.

Josh Boggi has just returned from training in Mallorca. On such a grey day, and with the queue for the dentist so long he decided to abandon it altogether, he must be tempted to turn round and go straight back to the Balearics. We sit by the window of a coffee shop and he tells me his story.

His surname – soft 'g', to rhyme with 'dodgy', 'podgy' or 'stodgy', three adjectives which could hardly be less applicable to a man so decent, so fit and so dynamic – is Italian. His grandfather came over from Tuscany after World War Two with his siblings: seven brothers and one sister. They all opened restaurants in the East End of London, which in itself sounds like the pitch for a comedy film or family drama. Josh's father served in the Royal Engineers for more than a decade, and for as long as he can remember Josh wanted to follow in his dad's footsteps and become a sapper (a combat engineer who, among other things, lays roads, builds bridges and clears mines).

In January 2004, aged just 17, he signed up and underwent basic training – phase 1, general training, to a base level of military competence, and phase 2, specific training for the Engineers themselves. He was then selected for 9 Parachute Squadron, an airborne detachment of the corps with a history so long and distinguished that you can chart much of Britain's wartime and post-war military history through its service records: the Dunkirk evacuations in 1940, the 1944 defence of the bridge at Arnhem, clearing the King David Hotel in Jerusalem after the 1946 Irgun bomb attack, the Falklands in 1982, rebuilding Rwandan infrastructure after the 1994 genocide, Bosnia and Kosovo in the 1990s, and of course three decades of the Troubles in Northern Ireland.

It was a history of which Josh was well aware. 'The minute you put the uniform on you feel proud. Grown-up.' He loved the British Army and everything it offered him. He'd always been a sporty kid, particularly keen on football ('I was a goalie. All the nutters play there') and ice hockey, the latter a craze sparked by seeing the *Mighty Ducks* movies. Now he could not only indulge his passion for sports and adrenalin but get paid for it too.

Every soldier who joins up itches for real combat, and there was plenty around for Josh. All British operations in Afghanistan went under the codename 'Operation Herrick', with each new order of battle receiving its own ordinal. Josh was first deployed as part of Herrick IV in 2006.

For six weeks nothing much happened. Then it all kicked off.

The 9 Squadron were sent in to Musa Qala, a dusty town in Helmand Province, to assist the Pathfinder platoon stationed there. The soldiers controlled a central compound of low cement and mud buildings surrounded by a 10ft wall, and a 10ft wall was nothing when the compound was surrounded by a maze of rubble-strewn buildings. Paradise for the Taliban militants using those buildings as cover and a nightmare for the men inside the compound, knowing they could be attacked from any direction and at any time.

Which is exactly what happened.

'I was 19 years old,' says Josh. 'The moment the first bullet flew past my ear, it was like, "shit just got real".' Every time the British troops dropped one militant, another two would pop up. It was like a nightmare pitched at the exact intersection of the Alamo, Rorke's Drift, a spaghetti western and a video game. The Pathfinders had been in Musa Qala some weeks already and were exhausted and jumpy, particularly at twilight – 'the witching hour', they called it – when they most expected the attacks to start again. They were running low on food, water and ammo, and they had no more batteries for their night vision devices. They needed resupply, but any kind of air support was out of the question: it was too easy for the Taliban to shoot down any helicopter which came near, and they'd all seen *Black Hawk Down*.

There was only one thing for it: a forced relief ground mission. A Danish squadron was on its way from Bastion, but it wasn't as if the Taliban were going to wave them through with open arms. Josh's men were tasked with clearing a way for the Danes, come hell or high water. It's 60 miles from Bastion to Musa Qala, but it took 9 Squadron and the Danes five days to make the journey, and even then it needed fixed bayonet fighting and six 1,000lb bombs on Taliban positions before they could break into the compound itself.

Hell of an introduction to war.

It was Josh's first tour of Afghanistan, but it wouldn't be his last. He went on Herrick VIII in 2008 and again on Herrick XIII in 2010, when he was deployed to Forward Operating Base (FOB) Khar Nikah. On the last day of the year, New Year's Eve, Josh was second-in-command of a search team sent out to clear a suspected Taliban compound. It was a patrol which, if not exactly routine, was hardly uncommon: get out, perform the task, get back in again. Simple enough.

But for Josh it all felt off, right from the start. Not by much – more a sense that the world had slightly tilted on its axis, that things were slightly out of alignment – but not by much was quite enough when it came to a place like Khar Nikah and the narrow margins between safety and danger, between life and death.

They went out of a different gate than usual.

Narrow margins.

The muezzin was calling the faithful to prayer at sunrise as always, but for once the ululations sounded menacing and ominous, sending a slow cold sweat crawling down Josh's spine.

Narrow margins.

Josh concentrated on the basics. Tread in the footsteps of the bloke in front of you. Keep your distance. Keep your eyes open. Keep looking. Never get complacent, not for a second. A second is all it takes. No one on Herrick XIII underestimated the Taliban. They were very good fighters (certainly those blokes who'd served in Iraq as well rated them far more highly than the Iraqi insurgents), their predecessors had seen off everyone from the Soviet Army back through the British in Victorian times and beyond, and they could rely not just on each other but also on what the Westerners called 'Tier Two' – those who weren't proper Taliban but helped them out with supplies, cover and so on.

The 9 Squadron liked to Grand National rather than mousehole: that is, they preferred to climb over walls rather than blast their way through them. Grand Nationalling was quicker, saved materiel and was less likely to advertise their presence. The problem with Grand Nationalling was that if the Taliban saw you doing it they'd shoot, and it was hard to shoot back when scrambling over a wall. So this time Josh's men went the explosive route: two half-bar mines and in through the breach point. Each time they marked the safe area, where they'd swept for mines, with white lines either side.

Narrow margins.

Mine, prime, breach ... Mine, prime, breach ... Watch the white lines.

The day slightly off; that strange sense of foreboding.

Josh took a step to the side ... Just one.

One was quite enough.

A beautiful cloudless day in the Golden State, warm enough for Sarah Rudder to be sitting outside by the pool even though it's not yet mid-morning. An all-American scene for an all-American girl, even one who grew up a long way from California: in the northern English town of Chorley, Lancashire, to be precise, where she played for Chorley Ladies' premier league soccer team and was top scorer for three seasons running. The Mia Hamm of Chorley? She laughs. 'Exactly that!'

But her heart was always in America, and from the age of 12 even more specifically set on the US Marine Corps. She'd seen them performing a silent drill, a dizzyingly slick routine of weapon handling, spinning and tossing performed without a word – the weapons in question being rifles with fixed bayonets, which provide obvious incentives not to mess up the catches. What captivated young Sarah was not just the beauty of such split-second timing but everything that came with it: the endless practice to make perfect, the discipline and confidence to execute it so flawlessly when it mattered, the absolute trust you had to have in your comrades and they in you.

She enlisted in the Marines as soon as she was legally able, in 2000 at the age of 17. But it wasn't plain sailing. She twisted an ankle so badly that she needed surgery, and on the way to hospital in Maryland for a post-operative check-up she was involved in a car crash which left her with a broken nose, ribs and scapula. But Marines are made of stern stuff, and Sarah was no exception. She was back in training as quickly as possible, and within a year was promoted from Private First Class to Lance Corporal.

Her promotion ceremony took place on a day as piercingly blue and bright as the one on which she's telling me her story: a late summer's day in Arlington County, at Marine Corps HQ, just opposite the Pentagon, 18-year-old Sarah, smart and proud in her dress uniform, her entire career ahead of her and the world at her feet. Friends and families in the audience, glowing as they choked back happy tears of pride.

An all-American day for the all-American girl.

A sudden roar so close and loud it made everyone jump. They were military people and they knew – they *thought* they knew – what that sound was: a ceremonial fly-by, a fighter jet opening up its throttles to make pure thunder. But fly-bys don't tend to take place in the nation's capital on a Tuesday morning.

A silver streak past their vision, an impact which shook their building like an earthquake, and then a fireball climbing high and fast in roiling clouds of orange and black. All in a matter of seconds before anyone knew what was happening.

It was 9.37 a.m. on 11 September 2001, and American Airlines 77 had just crashed into the Pentagon.

Newly promoted Lance Corporal Rudder and her colleagues swung into action. They sprinted across to the Pentagon and began performing basic triage on the injured: the walking wounded they sent to base corpsmen, the more serious they loaded onto tarp stretchers for the paramedics to take to hospital. Then they began to help the firefighters any and every way they could: bottled water for when they came out of the inferno gasping with thirst, new socks to replace the sweat-soaked ones inside their heavy boots.

Sarah did 12 hours' duty at the Pentagon, another 12 on patrol at Marine HQ, and then back to the Pentagon, where she had to pick her way through the mountains of flags and flowers left there. Running on adrenalin, she didn't sleep for three days straight. On the second day, when the building had been declared safe – or safe enough – she and her best friend, Ashley, joined the search and rescue team. They donned hazmat protective body suits and went inside, to the hideous twisted ruins, where the 757 had hit at a speed of more than 500mph. Their official mission was to locate and bring out 'non-survivors', a deliberately anodyne term which scarcely hints at the horrific sights Sarah and Ashley saw in there.

More than a decade and a half later, the California sun is not warm enough to keep her from shuddering as she remembers. 'The smell. Urgh! God, that smell … The smell of death. We had to sleep with the windows and doors open to try and get rid of it. The clothes we were wearing, we burned them, but it didn't do any good. The smell was still there in our skin.'

Even though her scapula was still healing, she'd taken her sling off – she couldn't do any lifting with it on. She and Ashley loaded corpse after corpse onto stretchers and brought them out: these people had families, and Sarah wanted them to have someone to bury. She lost count of how many bodies they handled. While walking backwards with one of them, Sarah got her left ankle stuck in a concrete barrier, which then fell and crushed it. Somehow she worked herself free, and was glad to find the damage didn't seem too bad. It wasn't hurting too much, and nor was her scapula.

That night, back at Marine HQ, her foot was so swollen that she couldn't get her boot off. And now the adrenalin was subsiding, her ankle was hurting, hurting really badly. Her scapula didn't feel too flash either, but her ankle was worse. It would get better, though. Wouldn't it?

It wouldn't. And it wouldn't be the end of her problems either. For Sarah Rudder, as for so many of her fellow countrymen in one way and another, 9/11 wasn't an end to anything. It was just the beginning.

Stephan Moreau joined the Canadian Navy because of a drunken bet.

Well, in a manner of speaking. He'd been out with some friends in a bar and, after a few drinks, told them that he wanted to serve his country and was going to the recruiting centre first thing the next morning. They laughed it off at the time and probably didn't even remember it the next morning. But Stephan did.

He wasn't one of those guys who'd always wanted to be in the military, the kind who left high school one day and joined up the next. He was 27 when he walked into the recruiting centre that morning in 2000: old enough to have done things with his life he knew now weren't for him, old enough to know what he really wanted.

He'd been brought up in Quebec City as the only child of a single mother, and sometimes the absence of a father grated – 'My mom did a great job, but something was missing. She was working so much that I had to learn to be independent and deal with my own problems. My character was definitely shaped by having to look after myself.'

It was shaped by sports, too. Stephan enjoyed baseball and athletics, but like so many Canadian kids, his real passion was hockey. 'It was hockey all the time. Outside rink in the winter after school and road hockey in the summer. I was shorter than most of the guys, but my speed and my feistiness made up for it.'

His hero, Calgary Flames winger Theoren 'Theo' Fleury, was cut from the same mould. At only 5'6" Fleury had been told repeatedly that he was too small for the big time, but his determination meant he ended up playing more than 1,000 games in the National Hockey League.

What job would allow Stephan to keep up his sport? Stephan's uncle had been in the Air Force, and 'he told me that 50 per cent of the time he was playing sports there! The military training was easy, especially boot camp. I was fit and I already had the discipline from playing hockey.'

He moved pretty much all the way across the country, from Quebec City in the east to Victoria in the west, and was stationed at CFB Esquimalt, Canada's main Pacific Coast naval base. It was a great place to live: right by the ocean, where he had always found his peace.

He served as Leading Seaman and Naval Communicator on the HMCS *Algonquin*, a destroyer which had been built in 1973, the year of Stephan's birth. The Canadian Armed Forces were busy after 9/11, and the *Algonquin* was no exception. Stephan patrolled the Gulf of Oman, checking out suspect vessels and boarding them, if necessary – 'We were the first warship to intercept terrorists. I'll always remember the buzz on the ship when we caught them.'

For those first four years on board the *Algonquin*, Stephan was happy: doing a job he loved and was good at, and feeling as though he was making a difference.

Then, in 2004, he was sent on a training exercise.

Those exercises were tough – three hours of sleep a night for three weeks, the dreaded red-hatted Sea Training Instructors waking everyone up in the middle of the night or making them start an exercise 20 minutes after going to sleep, that kind of thing – but of course that was the whole point of them. They were designed to test the sailors' reactions and decision-making when they felt like zombies.

In case of fire, sailors were supposed to wear a rebreathing system called Chemox. Speed in getting the equipment on was vital, so this was one of the crucial drills they practised. The first four men to the zone were to start putting on firefighter uniforms, the next four there were to help them. Stephan was one of the second four, so he began helping his friend, Joe.

Chemox used canisters full of chemicals. Stephan slotted the canister into the apparatus. There was a flash and a bang, and suddenly the canister was alight and was spewing toxic fumes and black smoke and flames into Joe's mouth and down into his lungs. He was screaming and Stephan and his colleagues were tearing the gear off him as fast as they could. But the apparatus was hard to undo, and in their desperation they got in each other's way. Even so it only took a few seconds, but a few seconds is a long, long time when a man is yelling for his life.

'It was screaming like I never heard before, it was awful.'

Joe was put on a helicopter and medevaced to hospital. Amazingly, given how horrific the incident had been, he recovered.

Stephan was not so lucky.

The vast shopping centre of Westfield Stratford City is almost empty at 9.30 in the morning. Most of its habitual clientele are either at work or still asleep. For Maurillia Simpson, 9.30 is the end of her day rather than the beginning. She works in the control room which ensures the security not just of the mall but also of the Olympic Park next door, and this week she's on night shifts.

'Simi' – everyone calls her Simi – was born and brought up in San Fernando, Trinidad's largest city, but for as long as she can remember she wanted to be in the British Army. There was no specific reason for this, no father in the services or anything like that – no father around at all for that matter, since Simi was brought up by her mum, a pre-school teacher, and her seamstress grandmother.

In 1985, the Queen came to San Fernando on an official visit. Simi was 10 years old at the time and her school was one of those chosen to line the route. Along came the Queen, smiling and waving the royal wave.

'I was convinced she was waving at me!' Simi says. 'Absolutely convinced. So I shouted, "I'm going to live where you live one day!", and the next thing I remember is this bang on the back of my neck from my teacher, trying to get me to shut up!'

Simi left home at 16 and went to Cascade, a suburb of Port-of-Spain, where she worked menial jobs and lodged with a family who became more or less her surrogate parents. She passed the exams for the Trinidad and Tobago Defence Force, but never got the call to begin training. But she was undaunted: those twin dreams of being in the British Army and living where the Queen lived still burned fiercely in her.

She landed at Heathrow on a freezing February day in 1999. 'This shows you how green I was, since I was dressed in shorts, T-shirt and shades. I had no idea where England was. I thought it was another part of the Caribbean, a quick island hop away, just like home. Then I looked out of the window of the plane and there were all these people in thick coats and you could see their breath in the cold air. I refused to get off the plane! "This is not England," I said. "Yes it is," the crew said. I wanted just to stay in my seat till the plane turned round and went back to Trini again. But of course I couldn't do that. Eventually the crew gave me about six spare blankets and I wrapped them all around me and shuffled into the terminal. I was staying with my auntie in Southall, and when I got there the first thing I said was, "Why didn't you tell me?"

'"Tell you what?"

'"Tell me that this place is so darn cold."

'"I thought you knew!" she said. "It's not exactly a secret."'

The very next day Simi went to join the British Army, swaddled in as many layers as she could find in her aunt's house. The nearest recruiting centre was miles away in Edgware, Barnet, but she found it, and by the time she returned to Southall that evening she had signed up to be a driver and communications specialist for the Royal Logistics Corps – contingent on passing basic training, of course.

She was 24 years old and this was her life's dream. That evening, Simi was the happiest person in London.

It wouldn't always be as easy, of course. 'The culture of the Army was very hard,' says Simi. 'There are times when you have to defend who you are and where you're from. When I joined I was the only black female in my regiment and I was older than the other NCOs [non-commissioned officers].

They couldn't understand what I was doing there or why I wanted to be there.'

Perhaps paradoxically, things got better in combat zones, where there's always a certain purity to life: there are only two types of people out there, the ones trying to kill you and the ones trying to keep you alive. Simi did three tours of Iraq with 2/8 Engineer Regiment, including the invasion in 2003 and the final troop withdrawal in 2009. She 'felt a real purpose' out there, particularly when it came to the humanitarian side of aid work and infrastructure reconstruction – water, electricity, schools, bridges. She was also an object of curiosity for many Iraqis, who had never seen a black woman before and 'always wanted to touch my hair and my skin'.

And she had her fair share of near-misses too. One night she led a 12-vehicle resupply convoy to the Black Watch regiment near Amarah, south-eastern Iraq: 'Black Watch were undercover, so you get to a certain distance and then they call you in on the radio. I saw a soldier come out. He must have been a sergeant major or a staff sergeant. He waved his hands, signalling us, so my commanding officer told me to verge off into the desert. After we'd gone a little way they came on the radio and told us to stop immediately and don't move. He hadn't been signalling for us to go that way – he was trying to tell us it was a literal minefield! My commanding officer said, "Private Simpson, put the tyres of the truck *exactly* where I tell you, just like you learned in training." At that point I thought: "Why did I have that dream when I was seven years old?"'

But that was small beer compared to the moment in Basra on Simi's second tour in 2007, when she saw two mortar shells flying towards her. She just about had time to shout 'Incoming!' before the mortars hit the wall next to her, bringing it down on top of her.

'I didn't know if I was dead or alive. I started to sing an old gospel song, "His Eye Is on the Sparrow", the one my surrogate mum used to sing to me in Cascade. I was thinking of her, I was trying to say goodbye.'

Buried under the rubble, her songbird voice cracking through effort and fear, Simi forced the words out.

His eye was indeed on the sparrow, because even as she sang, Simi could hear voices, colleagues calling her name: '"Simi," they were shouting, "we're not going to leave you, we're going to dig you out."'

Having survived the worst that Iraq could throw at her, Simi figured – perhaps understandably – that her next deployment to Germany would be easier. She was sent there in 2010 before a tour to Afghanistan and threw herself into training: she was always efficient, always on time, never late.

Just for one day, she should have been late.

Just once wouldn't have harmed. Just once might have saved her. She was coming back to base on her bicycle one night, bang on time as usual. Even a few seconds late would have changed everything.

She hardly saw him. Those mortars in Basra had taken an age to arrive in comparison. A local driver running a red light. No time for Simi to react. Just him and her, car and bike, and the squeal of tangled metal as they collided.

Fighting in Afghanistan is a seasonal affair. It eases off in the winter when the mountain passes are snowbound and ramps up again in the spring and summer. The latter, of course, brings its own problems to troops on the ground. The intense heat, well into three figures Fahrenheit, means soldiers have to carry vast amounts of water with them, and it can also play havoc with electronic equipment such as radios and microwave radar. Even tyre pressures have to be adjusted downwards to prevent blowouts.

By the time October 2008 came around, Mike Goody had been in the country for six months, watching the danger and the action rise with the heat and now begin to fall away slightly. He was deployed on Herrick VIII with the RAF Regiment's 1 Squadron. Despite its name, the regiment comprises ground troops rather than pilots: it's a specialist airfield defence corps whose members are known as 'rock

apes' after a 1952 incident in Aden when one officer acciden-
tally shot another after mistaking him for a hamadryas
baboon, known locally as a 'rock ape'.

The military ran in Mike's blood. His father had served
in Northern Ireland, and his godfather, Stanley Duff,
who was so close to the family that Mike simply called him
'Uncle Stanley', had been the youngest RAF squadron leader
in World War Two – 'He was a great man in himself, kind
to all, but to me he was more than a man could ever be. I
owe this man more than I could ever wish or have to give.
He was one of the main reasons that I joined the Royal Air
Force myself, not as a pilot like he was but as a Regiment
Gunner.'

And now here Mike was, on a day which though a few
degrees down on the sledgehammer heat of high summer
was still pretty hot. He was on patrol around Kandahar,
where the airfield served as NATO's main base in southern
Afghanistan. Sometimes it seemed less a military installation
and more a small town: the perimeter fence was 30km long,
and inside it were almost 20,000 soldiers and civilians from
a dozen different NATO countries.

The rock apes liked to go out in soft hats rather than hard
helmets whenever they could, knowing that hearts and minds
were easier to win over if you weren't dressed too much like
RoboCop. It was a fine line, and they knew that even with

the best will in the world they would never be able to fully convince the locals that their presence here was welcome. Whenever a patrol left the airfield they would see a sudden rash of kites in the sky: the local children signalling to the Taliban that the infidel were on the move.

Warfare starts young in Afghanistan.

And always the gnawing danger of the IED. It was a constant game of cat and mouse. Every time the Western soldiers found a way to detect or disable the devices, the Taliban changed their tactics: from pressure pads to phone signals, from phone signals to laser beams. You never left the base without thinking about them, without scanning the road for them, without doing everything you could to find them before they found you. Signs of digging, suspicious debris, a mound in the dirt that looked too exact to be natural ... You never stopped looking for those things.

And sometimes you could take every precaution imaginable and still find it wasn't enough.

Mike's patrol were a kilometre from camp, just far enough for anyone planting an IED to have been missed by the watchtowers standing sentinel on the airfield's perimeter. The patrol knew – because they always tried to think like the enemy – that if they were going to bury an IED somewhere, this was exactly the kind of place they'd have chosen. So they stopped and scanned the ground with metal detectors.

But when an IED is right up close to a vehicle, a metal detector won't work on it – it'll be too busy detecting the 4.5 tons of armoured vehicle nearby.

They put away their detectors, climbed back in the vehicles and set off again, with Mike driving the lead vehicle.

Mike was driving the lead vehicle right over the bomb.

A Skype connection across 10,000 miles, 11 hours' time difference and about three times that in temperature, and Darlene Brown from Brisbane laughs so readily and easily it feels as though she's in the same room as me. She's one of those people you can never imagine not liking.

Her dad had fought in Vietnam, a veteran of the famous Battle of Long Tan in 1966, when barely 100 Aussie soldiers holed up in a monsoon-lashed rubber plantation had defeated 1,500 Viet Cong. Darlene wanted to follow in his footsteps and sign up for the Army at 16, the earliest she was allowed, but he put his foot down: the Army, he said, was 'no place for a lady'.

Two years later, by now old enough to do what she wanted whether or not he agreed, Darlene joined the Navy. It was 1999, and right from the start she loved Navy life – loved it so much, in fact, that she volunteered for extra sea deployments in place of shore service, an attitude greatly appreciated by her senior officers.

It wasn't until much later that the effect of such a relentless schedule would become clear.

Darlene was assigned to the frigate HMAS *Adelaide* as a Communications and Information Systems Officer. In the aftermath of 9/11, when all eyes were on Afghanistan, the *Adelaide*'s concerns were closer to home. In October 2001, 100 nautical miles north of Christmas Island, it intercepted a vessel carrying more than 200 asylum seekers.

This wasn't the first time a Navy ship had been called into action this way, and the illegal immigrant issue was controversial, especially with a federal election only a month away. 'We decide who comes into this country and the circumstances in which they come,' said Prime Minister John Howard, and it seemed most Aussies agreed with him.

Politics or not, the *Adelaide*'s orders were clear: they were to 'deter and deny' the vessel entry to Australian territorial waters. A party from the *Adelaide* boarded the vessel and set it on a course back towards Indonesian waters. The situation grew tense. Some asylum seekers began sabotaging the vessel: 14 men either jumped or were thrown overboard.

In the confusion, there were rumours that the asylum seekers were also deliberately throwing children into the water in order to force the *Adelaide* to rescue them. The 14 men in the sea were fished out and put back on board the vessel; the 'children overboard' rumour turned out to be false. As it was, the vessel subsequently sank while under tow by the *Adelaide*, and all the asylum seekers ended up on board the frigate anyway.

It was only through a combination of chance and the professionalism of the *Adelaide*'s crew that no one had been killed. But the incident affected Darlene badly. It wasn't the only one to do so, nor was it a game-changer in itself, but little by little she was feeling her reserves ebbing away. Every time she came across a life-threatening situation – and there were some, of course there were, this was the Navy – her resistance was stretched thinner and thinner.

By 2004 she had been at sea almost constantly for three years, and she was changing – 'I was in the Gulf and I was starting to get angry. I wasn't the same person I was before. I was screaming my head off at people.' With the rages came the tears: long periods of uncontrollable sobbing, totally disproportionate to anything which could possibly have triggered them.

She needed help. But if she didn't know what was wrong with her, how could she know who to ask?

In 2016, when the BBC were looking for new *Top Gear* presenters, Bart Couprie (with tongue firmly lodged in cheek) put himself forward – 'I'm tall, balding, un-PC, slightly obnoxious, and I own a suitable wardrobe.'

Top Gear could have done much worse. Bart is funny, articulate and a good talker. But the BBC's loss is the New Zealand Navy's gain. At 49, he is still serving after 31 years.

He never wanted a normal nine-to-five job, and his father was in the Royal Netherlands Navy (the Dutch heritage is strong: Bart's full name is Bartus and his twin brother is Boudewijn), so a life at sea was a natural progression.

In those 31 years he's been stationed in many different places, including the South Pacific, South-East Asia and a 1999 peacekeeping stint in the Solomon Islands, 'which all went pear-shaped. We were playing a rugby match with the islanders, and not long into the second half we had to abandon it because a bunch of rebel groups were shooting at each other. Which was really annoying because though we were 13–8 down, we were coming back strongly.' Eighteen years on and he can still remember the score and the match situation.

Only a Kiwi ...

In Hawaii, he laid a wreath over the wreck of a New Zealand ship sunk by a Japanese submarine in World War Two. For Bart, history and the traditions of the Navy aren't adjuncts to his role, they're an integral part of it – the past inseparable from the present. From his first days in uniform at the local Sea Cadet Corps unit – 'old, scratchy, ex-Navy surplus, but a uniform' – he and his colleagues would march to the local cenotaph every 25 April, Anzac Day.

'During my first parades, I would fidget, look about and try to get a glimpse of what was going on. I noticed all the men – some aged in their seventies, some in their fifties and sixties – who would gather and talk, but at a certain moment their backs would straighten, their shoulders would square up and at the order to step off, they would begin to march. You could almost see the years fall away as they stepped forward, the bodies remembering the drill from so very long ago. There always was a sense that there were many more people marching than I could see. There was always a presence, in the pre-dawn darkness, that the fallen were marching with their old comrades.'

Bart's first Anzac Day parade was in 1979. He hasn't missed one since – 'I've paraded at Anzac services in places like Dargaville, Whakatane, Mt Maunganui, Browns Bay, Birkenhead, the Auckland Museum, Apia, and most memorably at the Kranji War Cemetery in Singapore.' And time has marched alongside him. When he started out there were World War One veterans still marching – 'Now they're all gone and even the World War Two vets are rarely seen.'

He remembers the medals those old-timers wore – 'Row upon row of medals. Always worn humbly, almost out of a sense of obligation rather than pride.' Over the decades he gained his own medals, for his length of service and peacekeeping missions like the one in the Solomon Islands, but he always felt that these baubles paled into insignificance compared to the ones from yesteryear, the ones 'awarded for a time when it seemed the whole world was aflame, awarded for years of combat, for the struggle for civilisation itself'.

Then one Anzac Day, before dawn, he had an epiphany. They were marching 'onto the hallowed ground at the Auckland Museum', and the number of serving personnel exactly matched the number of veterans: 'We halted on either side of the cenotaph and turned to face each other. They looked at us, we looked at them, and I imagined a mirror between us. In us they saw their past, and in them we saw our heritage. They gave us the traditions and the values that we in the military hold so dear. We gave them the knowledge that the ideals and values they fought and died for lived on in us.'

From that day on Bart saw his medals, the ones he had felt second-rate and undeserved, in a new light. He realised that 'they represent more than just my service. They represent all the values that I live by, and they are a touchstone to the past they fought in, and the future they left for us.'

But no matter how laudable the values, life in the armed services is often hard to reconcile with maintaining a happy and stable marriage. After more than two decades together, Bart and his wife split up – 'From a happy house full of family, I ended up in a small townhouse, with the cast-offs of my 22-year marriage strewn around me. Without knowing it, when my life started to unravel, I started setting myself goals. Goal one, keep a relationship with my children, which has been difficult, but rewarding. Goal two, try to have an equal and fair settlement. Goal three, buy a property (not easy in Auckland, but I did it!). As each hurdle came up, I set another goal to overcome it.'

He was about to come across the biggest hurdle of all.

In November 2014, still reeling from the effects of his divorce, Bart's future in the Navy – and by extension his entire life – was suddenly thrown into jeopardy.

Over the years he, like most men, had taken a 'perverse pride' in highlighting the times his body had almost failed him, like 'the minor leg infection picked up from a rugby field which flared up into a full-blown fever at sea, halfway between Papua New Guinea and Manila. X-rays later showed I was within millimetres of the infection reaching the bone, and that would have led to an amputation. A manly tale of a manly man doing manly things. Drain pint of lager, burp, refill, repeat.'

But this time was different. He noticed that he was having trouble urinating: his bladder never felt properly empty, and his stream was very weak. He went to see a doctor, who examined him and then sent him for a blood test, which indicated a prostate-specific antigen (PSA) count of 68.

Sixty-eight? What did that mean? Was it good? Bad? Normal?

'Put it this way,' the doctor said. 'We get concerned if a PSA's more than two.'

Mary Wilson lives in a spotless Edinburgh apartment with her partner, Judi, and their German Shepherd dog, Max. She brings coffee and biscuits. Max sniffs around me, decides that I pass muster, plonks himself down on my feet and promptly goes to sleep. On the far wall is a framed photo collage of men and women honoured for their services to Scotland. Just above the picture of Mary and Judi is one of Gavin and Scott Hastings, the nearest that Scottish rugby has to royalty. Decent company to be keeping.

Mary was always sporty: she played badminton and swam for Scotland, and represented Edinburgh at tennis. She joined the Queen Alexandra's Royal Army Nursing Corps in 1993 at the age of 29, and had only been in the Army a year when she was mentioned in dispatches for bravery while stationed in Hong Kong: not that 'bravery' gives any hint of what she actually did, which was to defend one of her patients against a drunken soldier from the Royal Scots, who beat up Mary so badly she needed a hysterectomy.

From Hong Kong she went back to the garrison at Catterick, north Yorkshire, and from Catterick, she went out to Bosnia. She was in charge of mental health for the entire British contingent out there, a responsibility deemed so onerous that her tour was three months rather than the usual six – 'It was terrible. There was a lot of alcoholism, a lot of underground drinking. It was the only way most people could cope with what they were being asked to do' – most infamously, as detailed in the TV series *Warriors*, being forced by their peacekeeping mandate to stand by and watch as atrocities were perpetrated against civilians they couldn't help, as even to evacuate them would have been deemed assisting in ethnic cleansing.

How many troops were drinking too much out there?

'Oh, about 80 per cent at least. Maybe more.'

Mary was on call round the clock. If a squaddie wanted to talk to her at three in the morning, she had to listen, no matter how tired she was or how much stress she was suffering – a considerable amount, unsurprisingly, having to take on all these soldiers' problems but with no one to really listen to her in turn.

The following year, 2000, she was thrown from her horse and into a wall during a course with the Royal Horse Artillery. Mary broke her cheekbone, two toes in her right foot and ripped her bicep muscle from her right shoulder. She needed two operations, but they didn't really cure her properly: in particular, she was having trouble holding and firing a gun, and if you can't pass the weapons handling course you're not much good to the Army.

The worst was yet to come. In 2004, while serving in Northern Ireland, she noticed problems with her balance and co-ordination – 'I kept falling over my left foot and I had blurred vision. At first they thought I had cancer, or a brain tumour.'

She was sent for tests.

The results came back: Mary didn't have cancer, and she didn't have a brain tumour.

Mary had multiple sclerosis.

CHRISTINE GAUTHIER, CANADA

Christine Gauthier signs all her e-mails 'Christine and Batak'. Who's Batak? An alter ego? Partner? No, Batak's more than that. Batak is her Labernese service dog (a mix of Labrador and Bernese Mountain Dog), and he's beside Christine in everything she does.

When she slides under the bench press bar, he's there with her.

When she gets in her specially adapted canoe, he's there with her.

He pulls her wheelchair, helps her keep her balance when transferring in and out of it, picks coins off the floor, nuzzles her when she's having a bad day, and a hundred other things besides.

'Without Batak, I wouldn't be here,' she states simply. 'He really, really saved my life.'

Christine's father was a cop, and to start with she wanted to follow in his footsteps: she went to police school in Montreal and became an officer in Quebec. But the lure of the Army proved stronger. She served with the Artillery for a decade, including two peacekeeping tours with the UN in Cyprus and on the Golan Heights in Syria.

Then, during a training exercise which involved jumping into a six-foot hole, she landed badly and damaged her knees, hips and back. Repeated surgery – she underwent eight operations in all – failed to repair the damage.

Christine found herself confined to a wheelchair.

She lost her job in the Army; she lost pretty much everything else too. Before the accident she'd been endlessly, relentlessly active: cross-country skiing, cycling, weightlifting, volleyball … You name it, she did it. Now she couldn't do any of that. She lost her spark, her joie de vivre. She'd still go and see the doctors three or four times a week, but the prevailing opinion on rehabilitation at the time was to do as little as possible in order to keep your condition from deteriorating still further. There seemed nothing they could do to get her better, and therefore nothing they could do to halt or reverse her long slide into total apathy.

'I was 10 years inactive in my house. Completely depressed and totally out of shape and left completely isolated.'

In 2010, the Winter Paralympics came to Vancouver. As Christine watched the coverage, it was like a light had come on in her head. These people were doing amazing things. These people had the same kind of disabilities she had: some of them, in fact, had it far worse. If they could do it, so could she.

She began to participate in adaptive sports. On the sledges in sledge hockey or out on the water in her paracanoe, she felt her strength coming back in great waves: not just her physical strength but her mental strength too, her will to overcome, her will to live.

Christine found a charity, the MIRA Foundation, whose mission statement said that they aimed 'to bring greater autonomy to handicapped people and to facilitate their social integration by providing them with dogs that have been fully trained to accommodate each individual's needs of adaptation and rehabilitation'. That described her and her needs in a nutshell, she reckoned. The Foundation agreed and they paired her up with Batak.

It was love at first sight.

She also received assistance from Soldier On, a programme run by the Canadian Armed Forces to help ill or injured personnel get back to as much normality as possible. And it was Soldier On who in 2014 asked whether she wanted to be part of the Canadian team which was going to the first Invictus Games in London.

The Canadian team was small, so they all got to know each other pretty fast. Just as importantly for Christine, the military shorthand they shared meant they could bypass the usual awkward questions they'd get from civilians. 'It's a certain type of people who join the Army,' Christine says. 'Sometimes those people don't fit in with the civilian world. But you see each other in the street and you just connect. I'm a reserved and shy person normally, not the kind to jump in a conversation, but when I'm in a military group that falls away.'

None of the team had any real idea of what they were going to. Unknown territory, it might be brilliant, or it might be garbage. Ah well … At least it gave her a chance to put on a Canadian uniform again, and at least they'd get a trip to London.

But it wasn't garbage, of course: it was brilliant. Only two Canadian competitors won two medals, neither of them Christine, but the experience made her hungry to do it again, to do it bigger and better. Like everyone else there, she was struck by Prince Harry's energy and enthusiasm. 'I'm not impressed with his title,' she says. 'But I am impressed with what he does with it. I'm admiring of the man he is.'

She threw herself into training for the 2016 Invictus Games in Orlando, which for her would be both a stepping stone and a time-out from her other main goal of that year: the Rio Paralympics. By now Christine was a multiple world champion in paracanoe, and had once qualified for a world championship final while paddling with a fractured elbow – 'When I go race, I know my mission, I know what I want to do. I just block everything out and do the best I can do. I have no boundaries, I just go for it.'

Paracanoeing is not offered at the Invictus Games. No matter, there were plenty of other things she could do there. The first day of finals, Monday 9 May, became Christine's own personal Medal Monday. Gold in the heavyweight powerlifting, gold in the four-minute indoor rowing and gold in the one-minute indoor rowing. A couple of days later, she added a silver and a bronze in swimming.

But Christine downplayed the personal merit of the hardware – 'It's not the gold medal around my neck that's important to me, it's Canada placing first. For me, the greatest moment is when my national anthem is being played.'

Besides, she knows that the officials got it wrong, at least in one small way. When those five medals say GAUTHIER Christine (CAN), there should be another name there too.

Not that the owner of that name cares too much. Not unless the medal comes with a dog biscuit, that is.

2

THIS PLACE OF WRATH AND TEARS

That single step Josh Boggi had taken meant that he was now standing on an IED.

The IED was a simple pressure-plate device built around two strips of metal held slightly apart. Each strip was linked by electric wires to a battery pack and a detonator set in the main explosive charge. The charge itself was made with farming fertiliser and housed in a cooking-oil canister. There was pretty much nothing in there which you couldn't build yourself from ordinary household items, which was why IEDs were so common in Afghanistan.

Josh's weight pressed the metal strips together, making a circuit which in turn activated the detonator and exploded the primary charge. The suddenly superheated gases expanded rapidly under the pressure – 'rapidly' meaning a shock wave travelling around 500 metres per second, blasting the canister and everything else in it (ball bearings, nails, bolts) into hundreds of pieces of deadly-sharp shrapnel. At the same time, the heat from the explosion set off a fireball and the blast wave caused a partial vacuum into which high-pressure air rushed back, pulling more debris and shrapnel with it.

All this happened in a split second, and Josh took the brunt of it.

Flesh and bone, no matter how strong and fit that person is, is no match for an IED. Josh was lifted clean off the road and hurled into a ditch – 'It felt like being punched really hard in the gut. Or winded in a rugby tackle, you know? I was just trying to suck the air back in. I had dust in my eyes and I didn't really know what was happening.'

His mates, on the other hand, knew exactly what was going on. They were on him in a flash. Through the shock and adrenalin, Josh gradually realised what they were doing. They had a tourniquet on each leg and another on his right arm: putting pressure hard on his arteries to stop him bleeding out right there in a dusty Afghan ditch.

'Fuck my legs!' Josh yelled. 'Are my bollocks still there?' One of his mates – this was no time to stand on ceremony, obviously – shoved his hand down the front of Josh's trousers and had a 'good old rummage around' – '"Yep," he said, "all still intact." Happy days!'

In the Salisbury coffee shop, we both laugh as Josh tells me this. Such a male reaction, to want to know the fate of your old boy above all else. Yet the laughter covers a serious point: ask any soldier what he'd prefer to lose ahead of and instead of his genitals, and the list will be long: arms and legs for sure, maybe eyes, maybe even life itself.

In that respect, Josh was lucky. Other soldiers at the time were being caught in blasts which weren't just taking out the perineal area where the two legs meet but going all the way into their pelvic cavities and severing the intricate urinary and other systems located there. An American naval surgeon deployed to Bagram Airfield three months after Josh's injury said, 'Nothing in my experience prepared me for the catastrophic nature of these injuries' – this from a former resident at a Level One Trauma Centre and seven years at hospitals in the US and Japan.

Every battlefield surgeon out in Afghanistan had tales of operating on men who'd wholly or partially lost their genitals, with all the scarring that entailed. The physical effects of losing testosterone-producing testicles were bad enough: among them, and in no particular order, osteoporosis, increased blood pressure, high blood sugar, excess body fat around the waist, abnormal cholesterol or triglyceride levels, cardiovascular problems, hormonal fluctuations and obesity.

But the psychological effects of such literal unmanning were even worse. You'd have no chance of kids unless you'd frozen your sperm beforehand. But in the rush to be deployed, who thinks of that? Even if they do, they might see it as a hostage to fortune, a superstitious irrationality: *If I do this, if I freeze my sperm, that means I expect something bad to happen to me, and if I expect it to happen, then it will happen.*

Sure, surgeons can do amazing things with penile reconstruction these days. To rebuild the urethra, which carries urine through the penis from the bladder, they use oral tissue from the patient's lips or the inside of the cheek, because it's hairless and used to being wet. For the outer layer of the penis they can graft skin from the thigh or groin nearby.

But rebuilding genitals and making them work properly – erection, orgasm and ejaculation – are two different things entirely. Besides, many surgeons who operate in this area are sex-change specialists, which in itself makes soldiers wary – *I ain't goin' to no sex-change doctor.* The bottom line was simple: losing a leg or an arm made you a war hero, losing your nuts made you a freak.

Yes, in that respect, Josh was definitely lucky. Not that he felt it at the time. One of his colleagues called in a medevac from Bastion, describing Josh's condition as 'T1' – 'the most serious you can be without being dead.' Some of the soldiers cleared a secure landing site for the helicopter. Others waited with Josh, cradling his head, keeping the tourniquets tight, keeping him conscious, keeping him talking, giving him grief for short-touring – 'Some people will do anything to get home early', 'You lazy bastard!', that kind of thing. Even – especially – in times like this, that was the Army way of showing you cared: there was nothing and no one you wouldn't take the piss out of.

The Chinook arrived, a giant airborne monster with vast rotors front and rear, which sounded like machine-gun fire as they blatted against the wind. Fading in and out of consciousness, Josh remembers his mates putting him on the Chinook and shouting 'Airborne!' His last coherent thought was, 'I'm still in this fight.'

The next thing he knew, it was a week later and he was in Birmingham's Queen Elizabeth Hospital (QEH). What he'd missed was a medical performance which was both mind-boggingly brilliant and yet entirely routine. Those were the standards to which Bastion's battlefield medics worked. World class was their baseline.

It was an unspoken rule that if you were still alive when the Chinook got you then you would survive – the medics were that good. More than that, in fact. For the Chinook crew, it was a question of pride that they delivered you to the field hospital in Bastion in better condition than they'd found you. It didn't matter how long or short the flight was, or whether they were being thrown about the interior like rag dolls while the pilots jinked and banked as they came in fast and low through incoming Taliban fire, the medics worked with the split-second efficiency of a Formula 1 pit-stop team. They weren't about just keeping you in a stable condition, they were already beginning that process of making you better, no matter how far off eventual recovery you were and how severe your injuries looked.

And Josh's injuries were severe, make no mistake. His right leg was stripped from the knee down, his left leg was back to the bone, and the underside of his ulna (forearm bone) was completely destroyed – 'It was the first time the surgeon had ever seen an ulna twisted so badly.'

At Bastion they put Josh in an induced coma, cut off all dead tissue, closed up his major vessels, cauterised the smaller ones and sent him on a transport plane back to Birmingham. It was in Birmingham where he regained consciousness, and in Birmingham where his dad, the man in whose Royal Engineer footsteps Josh had followed, broke the news as gently as he could.

Bad news: both Josh's legs were gone. His right arm would have to be amputated. And he'd broken his back.

Good news: he still had his nuts.

The staff at QEH kept Josh in intensive care for a week in order to be sure that he hadn't picked up any infections from the blast – the Taliban had been known to defecate on devices before covering them up, in order to add bacterial infection to the list of problems injured soldiers would have to deal with. When he showed no signs of infection, they moved him to the military wing. He wasn't the first triple amputee there, and he wouldn't be the last.

A week before he'd been a young soldier in the peak of health, doing the job he loved. Now he was a bedbound midget. It was quite an adjustment. There were some problems which were pretty obvious – phantom aches and pains in limbs which no longer existed, the psychological shock of needing to rely on someone else for the smallest of things – but also others which would never have occurred to anyone until it happened to them.

Temperature control, for a start. Much of the body's natural cooling system comes out through the soles of the feet and the palms of the hands. Josh had only a quarter of the normal amount of hands and feet left, not to mention much less surface skin area now his legs were gone. There were cases in which you could – and this was ironic, given the circumstances – you could have too much blood.

Then there was balance. You spent so much time lying down that it became hard to sit up, and when you *did* sit up, you were all out of kilter because you could no longer do what able-bodied people do instinctively and without thinking: move your legs and arms to ensure you're always in equilibrium.

'I had to accept that my life had changed for good immediately, and that wasn't easy.' But then again, Josh knew that if he'd wanted an easy life then he wouldn't have joined the Army. He began to tot up the positives. His head was fine, for a start. No mental problems – 'It helps sometimes, being an idiot' – which meant he could concentrate fully on returning to physical health. Those first six to eight weeks he did a lot of thinking, processing what had happened. He knew he had the capacity to do this processing, and he knew too that this ability was priceless. There were guys in the wing whose heads were messed up, and so they were fighting recovery on two fronts: mental and physical.

He thought of the Royal Engineers' motto: 'Adapt and overcome'.

His military liaison officer brought him McDonald's. The first Big Mac barely touched the sides, Josh ate it so fast.

Adapt and overcome.

Josh was happy to be alive, that was for sure. He wasn't one of those guys who thought they'd be better off dead, he was definitely happy to be alive. But alive meant living, not just existing. He wanted to be as normal as possible. But he had a wheelchair. A wheelchair wasn't normal for him.

Adapt and overcome.

Then one day he saw someone walk past the door to his room. It was one of the other soldiers, and he was wearing prosthetic legs. Josh called out to him. The man turned round and came into his room. Josh asked him everything he could think of about the prosthetic legs – how they worked, how they fitted, what did they feel like, where had he got them, and so on.

And finally, the most important question of all: 'Would they work for me too?'

The soldier looked at the stumps which had once been Josh's legs.

'I was just like that too,' he said. 'If they work for me, they'll work for you.'

Adapt and overcome.

A few months after coming home early from Operation Herrick XIII, Josh had another mission: Operation Walk Again.

Sarah Rudder could never escape that day in the Pentagon. Inside and outside, she carried it with her wherever she went. She could never escape it because it was part of her.

And that's right where she kept it, bottled up tight inside. For nine years she didn't tell her family she'd even been inside the crash site, let alone mention the unspeakable horrors she'd seen there. But even so it was becoming increasingly clear that something was badly wrong. She never lasted more than a year or two in any job. She did a college degree, but it took her nine years to finish it. She was finding it increasingly hard to deal with the usual minutiae of life, the things which most people navigate without even thinking about them.

Someone standing too close behind her in a line at the supermarket? No. Couldn't do it. Couldn't deal with it. So she became adept at going to the supermarket during the quiet times, when she could get in, do her shopping and get out with the minimum fuss and in minimum time.

Loud sudden noises? Definitely not. Which didn't make her much fun during Fourth of July celebrations.

How about continuous, repetitive noises? No, not them either, which was even harder when she had a son, who like all small children liked to repeat things over and over. For most parents that can get annoying, but for Sarah, it was a lot worse: sometimes she had to walk away before her head exploded.

She couldn't cope with fire or the smell of fuel, so backyard barbecues were out of the question too. All these things, little things which people took for granted and so found it hard to understand in her. Sometimes she felt she wasn't much of a mom to her small boy or much of a friend to her friends.

And so she did her best to avoid as many triggers as she could, but even that could be hard. Besides, the need to avoid triggers ended up imposing on her life quite as much as the triggers themselves did. She developed severe obsessive-compulsive disorder (OCD), endlessly labelling and organising things, forever tidying away the toys which her son had left strewn over the floor. She knew that it wasn't his fault – that's what small boys do – but she couldn't deal with it.

Anxiety hung above her like a cloud or twisted itself in her gut, even when she didn't have anything specific to be anxious about. As for sleep – what was that? Night after night she'd find herself staring at the ceiling in the small hours while the memories chased each other through her head.

That was the inside. On the outside, her ankle still hurt like fury. Pieces of bone had come loose and were tearing up the cartilage. Sometimes the pain was so debilitating that she honestly thought she couldn't stand it any longer. She was taking so much pain medication that she got kidney stones and had to have her gall bladder removed.

She had one operation on her ankle, then another, then another: five in all. They took cartilage from her knee and put in her ankle. They put metal rods in and then took them out again. They cut her Achilles tendon and lengthened it. They vacuumed out pieces of bone. Each time she thought, hoped, prayed it would fix the problem, and each time the disappointment came crashing down on her when she realised sooner or later that it was just as bad as it had ever been. Her ankle swelled up like an elephant's trunk, and sometimes she couldn't even put a sock on as the slightest touch made it feel like a firebolt.

Eventually she figured that if she was having treatment for her ankle, she should have treatment for her mind too. In 2010 she went to a therapist, who diagnosed her with post-traumatic stress disorder (PTSD) and suggested a couple of treatment methods. The first was prolonged exposure, where she was basically forced to deliberately expose herself to the triggers in the hope that she would eventually get used to them. The second was a sort of constant monologue, where she would record herself saying everything she saw, heard, touched, smelt and felt before listening to the recording at night while she slept.

Neither worked.

Just as frustratingly, her husband's job as a drone programmer meant that the family had to move frequently, and so each time they upped sticks and landed in a new place, Sarah would have to start afresh with everything that entailed –

new people who didn't know her history, a new school for their son, a new therapist for her.

In 2014, they moved to Temecula, south-west California. Another town, another doctor ... She'd had good doctors and bad doctors, ones she'd liked and ones she hadn't, but she'd never had one who really understood the problem. Not until now.

The doctor in Temecula examined her. He told her that the mental and physical sides of what she was going through were linked, which she already knew: the effort she had to put into managing the pain in her ankle directly affected her mental capacity to deal with her post-traumatic stress symptoms.

He could help her with the stress. He'd seen the kind of techniques she'd tried before, and he had some ideas as to what they could try differently: something a little leftfield, maybe, a little out of the box, not conforming to any prescheduled programme. Sure, Sarah said. She was good with that – it was worth a go at least.

As for the ankle pain, the doctor added, that was a different kettle of fish. If it hadn't got better after five surgeries, chances were it wasn't going to get better at all. Unless ...

Unless what?

Unless Sarah decided to amputate it, that was what.

* * *

It wasn't long after the Chemox incident that Stephan Moreau knew something was wrong with him – 'I became really agitated at work. I couldn't sleep at all, I started to isolate myself. I didn't want to do activities with my friends or family anymore. I started to withdraw from everyone.' When he and his wife were invited out to parties, he'd tell her he wasn't feeling too good, and while she went alone he watched sports on TV or surfed triathlon sites on the internet.

For someone like Stephan, usually so upbeat, this wasn't just a brief blip in his behaviour, it was a sea change in his very personality – 'I was passionate about my job, hard-working – and then the accident happened and I became this person that was going in the other direction. Instead of going up, I was going down and at a fast pace, too. I became very defensive and emotional as well. I was fragile, I've never been that fragile.'

He had a spell off the *Algonquin* in an onshore office – 'Not deliberately, just the way the rotation went' – and being away from where it had all happened helped him a bit. But soon he was deployed back to the *Algonquin*, where there was no escape. The incident was haunting him, brief intense flashbacks which railed his senses: the sight of the flames, the sound of Joe's screaming, the smell of the chemicals. He was afraid to be alone at night, because it was then that the memories, tangled and hallucinatory, haunted his nightmares, jolting him from sleep, wide-eyed and sweat-soaked, in the small hours.

He didn't tell anyone. Not a soul, not even his wife. He'd always brought himself up to deal with his own problems, with no father in his life and his mother always at work, trying to provide for him, and he wasn't going to change the habit of a lifetime. Besides, talking about this wasn't the kind of thing you were encouraged to do in the Navy. From inside and outside, the message was the same: be strong enough to deal with it on your own, be strong enough to put it behind you, accept that it happened and move on.

Stephan wasn't strong enough.

He needed help, and if he couldn't find it with a therapist then he'd find it in a bottle. He began to drink, but soon found it was a vicious circle: the more he drank, the more he needed to drink to keep himself numb, and even that didn't always work.

His superior officers may not have noticed his post-traumatic stress symptoms, but they did spot his drinking: it was affecting his work and making him put on weight. They told him to cut down on the booze. But he couldn't. They told him to stop altogether, and he couldn't do that either.

And so the bottom of the bottle became rock bottom in every way – 'I didn't have hope, or I didn't think I had hope.'

A few years after the Chemox incident, Stephan tried to kill himself with an overdose. 'Thankfully it didn't work out, and I'm still here today.'

Two separate investigations were held into the original Chemox incident. Both confirmed that the canister Stephan had used was defective. The investigators recommended removing the automatic emergency activation and overhauling the entire rebreathing system itself. Stephan was explicitly absolved of blame: it wasn't his fault, it had never been his fault. He knew that, but he also knew that logic had little or nothing to do with what he was suffering.

He began getting in trouble where he had never done so before – nothing huge, just little incidents of insubordination. But, combined with his drinking and substance abuse, for the Navy this was the last straw. In 2010 they offered Stephan an honourable discharge due to medical conditions – 'They pretty much told me: "Your career is over with us, but if you want, we are going to send you to a treatment centre before we release you."'

Stephan *did* want. Six years after the Chemox incident, he went to see a therapist. Their first priority was to deal with his alcohol and substance abuse, but the moment he told her what had started it all off, she smiled. 'I've seen more than 10 people from that single incident come through these doors,' she said. 'I've seen so many that I actually put the firefighting kit on and did that section of the training to try and understand it from the position of all you who were there.'

For Stephan, even though his naval career was all but over, it felt like a strange sort of deliverance. 'So I'm not alone?' he said.

'No,' she replied. 'You're definitely not alone.'

The impact of car against bike knocked Maurillia Simpson out cold, but only for a few moments. When she came round she was under the wheels of the car, and the first thing she did was get to her feet – 'I got hit and I got up, jumped up like nothing had happened.' She was about to deploy to Afghanistan and nothing was going to stop her, least of all some fool who'd bust a junction.

They wanted to take her to hospital. No, she said, she was fine. They insisted: hit by a car and knocked cold, even momentarily, she had to go whether she wanted to or not. And now the shock was wearing off and the pain was taking over, she knew they were right, and she knew too that she didn't want to go to hospital for fear they'd find something which would mean she wouldn't be able to go to Afghanistan.

The doctors examined her and took X-rays. She'd ruptured the whole left side of her body: her femur was so badly damaged that it would need realignment surgery. Afghanistan? Don't be daft. She should worry about walking properly again, not going to a war zone. Afghanistan was out of the question. They put her left leg in a cast which stretched from her groin to her ankle.

Simi was furious, the kind of fury which came so hard and fast and overwhelmingly that it threatened to submerge her. She was furious at the driver, she was furious at herself for having been in the wrong place at the wrong time, she was furious that her buddies were going off to Afghanistan without her, she was furious that she'd be stuck in Germany on her own, like Simi-no-mates, learning to walk again as though she were a damn toddler.

She hadn't seen the worst of it yet.

That groin-to-ankle cast would in the end stay on her for an entire year. The doctors cut her femur and reset it with metal pins, but the bones refused to fuse again properly and the metal wouldn't hold. The Army sent her to the Defence Medical Rehabilitation Centre (DMRC) at Headley Court in Surrey (whose work is explored more fully in Chapter 3), where she underwent four separate physical rehabilitation courses. In between she was stationed at the Royal Artillery Barracks in Woolwich, south-east London, and she was there when her colleague, Lee Rigby, was run down and murdered by two Islamic extremists on a nearby street in May 2013, a killing so brutal that it reverberates through the nation's psyche to this day.

Headley Court did what it could for Simi, but it wasn't enough. In 2013 she received a call from her commanding officer. 'He asked me, "Are you sitting down?" I said I was. He told me that the rehab tests showed I wasn't improving, and that there was only a certain amount of times you could go back. I said, "No, sir, you can't do this."'

But Simi was being medically discharged. She couldn't even be given a desk job, as everyone in the Army has to be able to walk a mile and a half and leave a building unaided, and she was now using a stick full-time.

It was November 2013. Simi's Army career was over. More than that her dream, her vocation, her life's work was over. She felt robbed and cheated, like she had nothing else to live for – 'I didn't see myself as being anything else but a soldier, because that's all I ever wanted to do.'

The Army gave her a basic invalidity pension but – her three tours in Iraq notwithstanding – not a war pension, as she wasn't technically at war when the accident happened. She applied for accessible council accommodation, but the waiting list was more than a year, Forces or not.

This wasn't a sideshow to her recovery, it was central – 'What people might not realise, as I didn't, is housing's direct effect on mental and physical well-being. Without a fixed address, no surgeon would consent to perform the operations I desperately needed to move forward. Where could I have gone afterwards to mend? My doctors weren't convinced the sofa of a friend was an appropriate place to get better. And nor were my friends.'

But that – friends' sofas – was all she had. It was better than being on the streets, but a long way off what she needed to help her recover, both physically and mentally. 'When you're without a home, or in a home that poorly suits your needs, the preoccupation and panic about your situation smothers your thinking. It becomes impossible to pick yourself up, look forward and reconfigure your future. It's also virtually impossible to find a job, when most employers want to hire someone with predictable living arrangements.'

And then, in this, her darkest of hours, her phone rang.

Mike Goody had been trapped under his vehicle for an hour and a half, and as far as he was concerned, enough was enough. It wasn't the pain in his shattered left ankle which was bothering him the most, it was the fact that his vehicle – this 4.5-ton monster, which was now held off the ground by 22 separate jacks; yes, 22 – that his vehicle had been the lead one in the patrol convoy, and he'd been driving it. That meant it was his own fault he was here, his own fault that his mates were doing all they could to get him out, and most of all, it was his own fault that they were all in danger of being attacked by the Taliban, out here a kilometre from their base at Kandahar Airfield.

A kilometre was hardly anything at all. On a good day he could run it in around four minutes. Right now, however, it might as well have been the other side of the moon, and the people inside that base eating at TGI Fridays and doing spin classes in the gym and all sorts, they seemed as though they came from another life entirely.

Mike was putting his mates in danger, and that just wasn't on.

More than a century before, when in the flat circle of time round these parts the British had been fighting the Afghanis, just as they were now, Rudyard Kipling had written a verse in his poem 'The Young British Soldier', which pretty much every man out here could recite word for word.

When you're wounded and left on Afghanistan's plains,
And the women come out to cut up what remains,
Jest roll to your rifle and blow out your brains
An' go to your Gawd like a soldier.

Mike had a pistol rather than a rifle, but the intent was the same: he'd blow out his brains, his mates could stop worrying about crushing him with the weight of the vehicle, and they could load up his body and get back inside the airfield before anything else went wrong.

He reached for his pistol. It would be quick and easy, a single shot before anyone could react. They'd be horrified, sure, but they'd understand.

Mike's fingers closed round thin air. His pistol wasn't where he thought it was. It must have been knocked somewhere else in the impact of IED blast on armoured vehicle. With the limited movement he had, he scrabbled around with his hand, desperately trying to get hold of his sidearm.

He couldn't find it.

It was another hour and a half before they could winch him out from under the vehicle. He was conscious the whole time. His ankle was in a bad way: he'd broken every bone in his lower left leg apart from his big toe. No more soldiering for him, not on this tour at least. He was back at Selly Oak within 24 hours and spent the next four months there. They operated repeatedly on his leg, securing it with pins, plates and screws.

The surgeons there were becoming increasingly accustomed to the unique patterns of blast injuries. In fact, blasts are a combination of three distinct types of injury: penetration, blunt trauma and pure blast. With every wounded soldier who came back they became more adept at the treatment. It was a ghoulish aspect of surgical medicine, that at certain places and certain times you can become a world expert in a given field simply because you're being given so much practice in it. The staff at Belfast's Royal Victoria Hospital found something similar in the 1970s and 1980s, when the IRA's habit of 'kneecapping' people – shooting them in the kneecaps – led directly to the Royal Victoria becoming the 'go-to' centre for knee reconstruction, not just in Great Britain but much of Europe too.

Mike had never met Sarah Rudder, but there was a remarkable similarity between their conditions: not just their ankle injuries, but what was going on in their heads too. Like Sarah, he began to suffer post-traumatic stress symptoms – 'I had moods where I would be aggressive. It was a pretty dark time. I shut out my friends and family. You try not to make too big a deal out of it, but inside it's tearing you apart.'

Fireworks would set him off just as they did her, though in his case it was exacerbated by the fact that the main period for firework displays in Britain (apart from New Year's Eve) falls around Guy Fawkes Night in early November, which came hard on the heels of the anniversary of his accident. At times it felt as though any loud noise would trigger him – 'I was in Tesco once and someone dropped a can of baked beans. In a flash I was flat on the floor on my belt buckles, shouting, "Incoming!" Everyone was looking at me like I was nuts.'

And also like Sarah, there was a direct correlation between his leg's refusal to heal and his ongoing mental trauma. He began drinking to numb the physical pain – he was already on 'mind-boggling' painkillers such as ketamine, which is also used as a horse tranquiliser – and this in turn made his stress symptoms worse.

Even after leaving Selly Oak, he needed repeated operations on his ankle: 14 of them, in fact, over a period of two and a half years. In trying to take the weight off his bad leg as much as possible, he was walking poorly, damaging his knees, hip and lower back. His posture and mobility were all over the place. Solve one problem and cause three more.

In 2011 a surgeon gave him the news straight: 'He told me I might have to have another two years of operations, with no guarantee of success at the end of it. I knew what I had to do.'

He looked the surgeon straight in the eye. 'Take it off,' he said. 'Take it off below the knee.'

It was a year after her symptoms – the rages, the crying jags – first developed in earnest that Darlene Brown was medically discharged from the Australian Navy. After so long away at sea, so long constantly on the move, she went in the diametrically opposite direction and retreated to the place she felt safest: home.

She tried to remain connected, even in small ways. A few visits to psychiatrists, which didn't do any good. A friend of hers had a son serving in Afghanistan, so she sent him a parcel. Then she began sending his friends parcels too – 'I became obsessed with sending parcels. I reckoned most people had no idea what life was really like for them out there, and so I wanted to help.'

But in general 'retreating home' meant just that. Sometimes she wouldn't even go outside the house for two or three weeks at a time, let alone beyond the garden and the front gate. Rather than go to the shops, she got as much stuff delivered as possible. When she *did* dare to step through that gate, she would conduct a full-scale risk assessment beforehand. She felt she was going mad and she had no idea why. She became paranoid that she was being watched and so she had a six-foot wall built, blinds installed so that no one could see in and three locks put on the door – 'I was an island without a moat.'

And in the way that so many people can do when suffering with behavioural-altering conditions, she managed to spin it so that to the outside world at least nothing seemed wrong. She set up in business as a masseuse, which meant that clients had to come to her house and that she could work on them for half an hour or an hour at a time without needing to say much. They'd tell her their problems, the intimacy of the massage table loosening their inhibitions, and she'd just respond noncommittally while crying silent tears and wanting to scream, 'YOU THINK YOU'VE GOT PROBLEMS? I'LL GIVE YOU PROBLEMS!'

She was angry because she couldn't feel happy, no matter what she did. Even items on the news could set her off – 'Just to survive the day was an achievement.' Life was chunks of 12 hours, no more. Get to sunrise. Get to sunset ... Get to sunrise. Get to sunset ... There was no question of doing anything other than that, anything wider or more exciting. And the more she stayed in, the more she walled herself away, the more fearful she became of ever breaking out of that mould – 'There was just this constant white noise in my head. You think people could see that, but of course they couldn't.'

Couldn't, or wouldn't? Certainly many people suspected the latter, at least when it came to the armed services. As Stephan Moreau had found on Vancouver Island, men and women in uniform weren't good at dealing with what they couldn't quantify, especially when it began to smell of weakness too. In some ways it was even worse for women, who'd worked harder than the men to prove themselves in a male-dominated world and now didn't want to be the one to let the side down by going to the doctor with psych issues.

There was glory in heroic acts of battlefield bravery but there was no glory in post-traumatic stress, no medals for just getting through the day in one piece, no attempt to take on and defeat an enemy which came in the form of thick living-room blinds shutting the world off from Darlene, and Darlene off from the world.

Then one day she saw an officer on TV. He was talking about PTSD. Darlene stared at him, open-mouthed. It was like looking in a mirror. Everything he said, everything he was describing, literally *everything*, he could have been talking about her. It was the first time she realised what was wrong with her.

Now all she had to do was take the first step to fix it.

The veterans support network Mates4Mates – the concept of 'mateship' is at the heart of what it means to be an Aussie, civilian and military alike – had its headquarters in Brisbane. It offered services in five key areas, one of which was psychological support. Darlene knew she needed to go there. From her home in northern Brisbane, it was 15 miles – half an hour's journey, more or less. Most people wouldn't think twice about it.

Most people hadn't been through what Darlene had been through.

She had to go.

Get off the sofa, Darlene.

She couldn't bring herself to go.

Leave the house, Darlene.

She had to go.

Walk to the bloody car, Darlene.

She couldn't bring herself to go.

Start the engine, Darlene.

Had to. Couldn't. Had to. Couldn't. Had to, couldn't, had to, couldn't, had to …

Had to.

For Bart Couprie, the next stage after being told that his PSA was, oh, 30 times or so the normal amount was a transrectal ultrasound guided prostate biopsy – 'It's as unpleasant as it sounds, yeah.'

A week or so later, the specialist asked him to come back in. Bart was in the early stages of a relationship with a woman named Jude. Those first few weeks and months were heady with excitement and the all-consuming joy of finding out about another person, but they were also delicate and fraught with danger, particularly when emerging from the bruising pain of a divorce. If there *was* something wrong with Bart, how would Jude react?

Well, there was something wrong with him, and it was exactly what he had feared.

'Yep,' the surgeon said, 'you've got prostate cancer.'

So much for it being an old man's disease.

As for Jude's reaction, it was threefold. First, she burst into tears. Then she hugged Bart. And finally she told him that he was moving in with her, *right now*, no ifs or buts, didn't matter how early in their relationship it was, and he had to get off his prostate-cancered arse and make it happen, and they were going to beat this thing together.

Cancer should have taken Jude on instead – it wouldn't have stood a chance.

CT and bone scans indicated that Bart's cancer hadn't yet reached his lymph system. He was put on a course of external narrow beam radiation with androgen deprivation therapy (ADT). The idea behind this was to shut down his body's production of testosterone, which in turn would – hopefully – stop the cancer in its tracks.

As so often with medical terms, it gave scarcely a hint at the trauma behind the names. ADT is more or less chemical castration, albeit temporary and reversible. It can cause fatigue, lowered libido and erectile dysfunction: a less aggressive form of unmanning than the kind Josh Boggi was so fortunate to have escaped, but unmanning nonetheless. For Bart, having a finger up his anus for the prostate examination wasn't to be the worst of it, not by a long way.

Back when homosexuality was illegal, chemical castration was often the punishment for those who were caught, among them the British scientist Alan Turing, whose cracking of the Enigma code had done so much to win World War Two for the Allies. 'Punishment is what I call it too,' says Bart. He had the first injection a month after being diagnosed, and then one every three months afterwards. The narrow beam radiation therapy – well, that was 'just the icing on a pretty shit cake'.

And in the list of ADT bingo, those side-effects he was warned about, pretty much every one of them came to pass.

Erectile dysfunction? Check, though 'Luckily I still retained some function, enough to complete the act at least.'

Hot flushes? Check. 'Saved a fortune on home heating.'

Loss of body hair? Check. 'Buggered if I know where it's gone. Got some regrowth on my head, though. Go figure.'

Weight gain? Check.

Loss of muscle mass? Check.

Joint pain? Check.

Mood swings? Check.

Depression? Check. And in some ways this was the hardest of all to deal with. He had 'a bit of a breakdown' and was put in the care of a psychiatrist. His GP suggested antidepressants, but Bart flat out refused – 'It was drugs that got me here in the first place.' He'd have to find another way round the depression.

He chose to do two things: he chose to exercise, and he chose to proselytise.

* * *

The first thing Mary Wilson thought when told that she had multiple sclerosis (MS) was that it was a disease of the people she'd nursed, those poor souls who were bedridden and incontinent, who needed catheters and whose bodies were wracked with spasms they couldn't control. MS wasn't the kind of disease she could get, not her. She was too young, too healthy, too fit – 'I thought I'd rather not be on this earth if I have to be that person. I went outside in tears.'

She had a good cry and then pulled herself together and took stock. There were two choices, she knew: go on or go under. 'Do I let this beat me?' she thought. 'No, I don't. Fuck this!' Told that running – which she'd always hated – might help, she began to do 10K races, and she and her partner Judi (and sometimes Max the German Shepherd too) started climbing the Munros, the Scottish mountains which stand more than 3,000 feet high.

There are 282 of them, boasting names so exotic they could have come from Tolkien or Shakespeare – Ben Lomond, Cairn of Claise, Glas Maol, Schiehallion, Spidean Mialach, the Devil's Point and the clue's-in-the-name Inaccessible Pinnacle – and to 'bag' the lot of them is a well-recognised and considerable feat. 'I didn't want to be that person I'd seen in the bed. Anything but that. I took a new look at life and got even more determined.'

There are three main types of MS, and Mary was initially diagnosed with the most common and least serious, relapsing remitting. Her symptoms would come and go, rise and fade. Sometimes she'd be fine, other times, and with little warning, she'd have mild relapses which could last a few days or weeks, and would leave her feeling exhausted and low on confidence and self-esteem – 'Each day is different when you have MS. You get those difficult times when mood swings and frustration are terrible. The fatigue, pain, memory loss and lack of co-ordination can make life extremely hard.'

But she could stay in the Army, and that was the main thing. In 2009 she was told she would be deployed to Afghanistan as the non-commissioned officer (NCO) in charge of the mental health team out there, but only if she could still pass the weapons test. She couldn't hold a rifle because of her shoulder injury, and MS was wearing away her co-ordination and finger strength so it was hard for her to fire a pistol. Undeterred, Mary asked a friend in the Special Forces to help her with the training – 'I just kept practising and passed the test.'

Afghanistan was every bit as hard as she thought it would be. The second night she was there, staying at the Kandahar Airfield, one of the local Afghan workers inside the camp drove his car at her – a similar fate to that which would befall Maurillia Simpson in Germany the following year, though Simi's was an accident and Mary's was deliberate.

'He was trying to kill me. I've no idea why, I'd never seen him before in my life.'

She ended up with sepsis from fragments of metal in her thigh and buttock, lodged there while diving out of the way, and when she woke up in hospital she found a Taliban member in the bed next to her – 'Yes, we'd treat them too when they were injured, and I knew that, but it still gave me a hell of a shock! That was tough to deal with, but I just got on with it.'

Mary got to know the rhythms of camp life in all their workaday morbidity. When a medevac helicopter came in, she could tell simply by the sound of its engines whether its cargo was alive or dead: if the soldier was still alive, the 'copter would touch down for only a few seconds, just long enough to get him off and on his way to the field hospital, but if he was dead then they might linger on the ground for a minute or two. And sometimes, unbearably, they would find Afghan babies left outside the main gates of the camp, 'tiny wee mites' covered in burns after air attacks and dumped there as if to say, 'This is your problem now.'

There was no alcohol in Bastion, so Mary didn't have to deal with the underground drinking which had been how her men had coped in Bosnia, but the mental challenges for the

British troops out there 10 years on weren't any less serious: how to deal with the constant threat of attack, how to process seeing your mates wounded and killed, how to keep yourself from worrying about families you knew were worrying about you, and so on. She spent many hours talking these things through with the men and women, trying to 'give them support and the tools needed to go back out to do their jobs and function properly'.

Afghanistan was to prove her last major deployment. In the end, it was a simple rule change which meant she could no longer pass the weapons handling tests, and in 2012 she was medically retired as a staff sergeant after 20 years' service.

But Mary was not finished yet – not by a long way.

SÉBASTIEN DAVID, FRANCE

Many Frenchmen like to talk of their attachment to the land, but for Sébastien David the sea has always been just as important.

When he joined the French Navy in 1997 at the age of 19, his aim was to become a member of the Naval Special Forces. He didn't have to wait long: just a year, in fact, before he was assigned to the assault team. After five years in Special Forces he moved into Protection and Intervention.

Sébastien's deployments took him to, among other places, Yugoslavia, Kosovo, Lebanon and Djibouti. Along the way, he picked up a number of injuries, coincidentally all spaced three or four years apart. One to the shoulder in 2001. One to exactly the same spot in 2004. ('I got a few screws and everything went back to normal.') One to the knee during an exchange with Lebanese commandos in 2008, after which he 'got a few more screws, then went back to business once again'. Finally in 2011, during a night exercise he fell heavily, resulting in lower-back trauma. His days of active frontline service were over.

'For the physical rehabilitation, I went to two large rehabilitation centres in France and got on medical leave for several months. As for the psychological rehabilitation, it was difficult at the beginning. I asked myself, "What will I become? What will I do?" But my wife helped me.'

Sébastien is now an instructor at the marine rifle school in Lorient, a city on the Brittany's Atlantic coast which is known as the 'five-port city' as it has separate ports not just for the military but also for commercial fishing, cargo, passenger ferries and yachts.

As with many competitors from various countries, Sébastien first heard about the Invictus Games via national organisations set up to help injured servicemen and/or promote sport within the military: in his case, the CABAM (La Cellule d'aide aux blessés et d'assistance aux familles de la Marine) and the CNSD (Centre National des Sports de la Défense). 'For me the military missions were over, but thanks to sport I still had goals.'

He went to Orlando in 2016 – 'I was able to defend the colours of France during the wheelchair basketball, rowing, swimming and archery. In the last of these I won the silver medal with my friends Captain Eric Baudrit and Adjutant Raphaël Perriraz. The atmosphere was incredible, and many families were present. It was magical. We don't have that in France! This love for the military is unreal.'

As for the best bit – well, that was easy, and it wasn't the silver medal: 'The best for me was the look in the eyes of my children. Because to them I was Superman. During the Invictus Games, all warriors are the stars. The Games allowed me to live a strong emotional and fantastic human and collective adventure. It helped in showing that the warriors are "the masters of their fate".'

It's a sentiment echoed by his teammate David Travadon –
'Please, no pity. We are strong, alive and determined. Many of
our friends are no longer with us: they departed too early, we
continue on for them. We are probably a little different now, but
what is normality? We are still soldiers. We give everything for
our country, for freedom, but we don't claim your thanks. We just
expect you to consider us as you would everyone else. It's the
nicest present you can give us.'

3

BLOODY BUT UNBOWED

Just outside the point where London finally stops sprawling, hard up against the M25 orbital motorway, which encircles the city like a 117-mile-long belt and carries more traffic than any other road in the country, is a late Victorian mansion which plays host to some of the most advanced rehabilitation programmes in the world.

It's only three miles from Leatherhead station, half of them through country roads, whose peace and quiet seem incongruous so close to the city. Farmhouses sit nestled in valleys of gently rolling green: a barn has been repurposed as offices for a digital media company keener on using exclamation marks than capital letters.

And then at the end of the road is Headley Court, which would be a beautiful but rather typical stately home – bay windows edged with ivy, manicured gardens, topiary hedges, arcing gravel drives – were it not for the soldiers at the gate, who check my driving licence against both my face and the details they already have for me, or for the signs which read 'COUNTER-TERRORISM RESPONSE LEVEL: SEVERE' and warn that the Official Secrets Act applies on these premises. Headley Court may be a medical establishment but it is a military one too, and the reminders are everywhere you look.

Built in 1899, it was originally a private home, but even then its connections with war were never far away. It was owned by Walter Cunliffe, who, as Governor of the Bank of England during World War One, was instrumental in both calming the markets at the outbreak of war and later liaising with the American government during their entry into the fighting. In World War Two it served as headquarters for units of both the British and Canadian armies, and immediately after the war it was used as a medical rehabilitation centre, first for the RAF and then for all three services, a role it maintains.

Headley's motto is *per mutos* – 'by mutual effort' – and the words are not hollow ones. Civilian contractors work alongside military personnel: patients are expected to give everything to their recovery and help the staff in the same way the staff help them. No one at Headley does things on their own – they're all in it together, and they all take visible and genuine pride in what they do.

Take Mark Thoburn. He works for Blatchford Services, a civilian company which makes and fits all the prosthetic limbs used here. When he started in 2006, he came in one afternoon a week, and he was the only Blatchford employee on site. Two years later, with the Afghan insurgency ramping up and the IEDs ripping limbs off more and more soldiers, there were seven people working five days a week. One day, he says, they might be back to one – the number of new arrivals is slowing now that Britain has withdrawn from combat operations in Afghanistan and Iraq – and he's determined he'll be that one.

'Best job in the world,' he says. 'Honestly, it is. To have the state-of-the-art stuff we have here, and to be able to do it for young men who still have their lives ahead of them, I just love it. If I was working on the NHS, I'd be fitting the most basic equipment to pensioners who've lost a leg to diabetes. Now, that's rewarding in its own way, of course, but the NHS just haven't got the resources to do any more than the minimum. We get you back to normal, or the nearest to normal we can. We're always being challenged here – "OK" is not nearly good enough. I can give these boys the very best there is. And get the piss taken out of me in return, of course.'

He rolls up his trousers: the bottom half of his right leg is artificial. 'Motorbike accident. One leg, below the knee: as far as most of the guys I see are concerned, that's nothing. I'm a pretend amputee.'

The way he describes his work makes it sound part science and part art. The first thing he does whenever a new patient comes in is fit them for their prosthetics. Prosthetics generally come in two parts: the socket which fits onto the stump, and the 'leg' which fits onto the socket.

But first things first. Onto the stump goes a suction liner of varying thickness, from 2mm at the top to 14mm at the bottom, where the stump will rest in the socket. Then Mark takes a cast of the leg, which he modifies with hand tools, and makes a diagnostic socket to check the fit. The socket is transparent at this stage, so he can see how the stump sits in it. It has to be tight enough to keep the soft tissue from moving around, tighter than you might think comfortable, but as far as prosthetic sockets are concerned, tight *is* comfortable. A badly fitting socket can be agony: imagine the worst-fitting pair of shoes you've ever had rubbing against a part of your flesh which itself has undergone savage trauma.

When Mark's happy with the fit, they make the socket for real. There's a workshop on site, full of bustle and good-natured banter. It takes a few days to make a socket, which is then taken back to the patient for fitting and adjustment. The sockets are built high up the back of the legs to help with weight bearing – 'Rather than get someone to put their weight through the end of the stump, we make sure most of the load's borne by their ischial tuberosity.'

By their *what*?

'Their arse.'

Sockets come in any number of patterns nowadays. Options available to the discerning amputee at Headley include the Union Jack, camouflage patterns, the V for Vendetta mask, skulls, a fake wood inlay and a rather fetching bright pink.

Now come the legs, clipped into the sockets with pin line locks. Single amputees, who still have one working leg, obviously need an artificial leg which matches the length of the real one. For bilateral amputees – those who've lost both legs – the process is different.

For a start, they have to learn to walk again from scratch, which brings with it questions of falling and balance. They therefore start on 'stubbies' – short, straight legs with no knee joints, which keep their centre of gravity low. Most amputees spend four to six weeks on stubbies before graduating to long legs. Many people hate them, at least to start with, because stubbies make them look like dwarves.

But the stubbie is a grower. Even when amputees have mastered long legs, often they wear stubbies around the house, just as able-bodied people wear slippers. Stubbies are also pressed into service as drinking and dancing legs, when balance is both important but impaired.

Once Mark and the physios are satisfied with the patient's core stability, hip and pelvis control, they move onto 'long legs' – 'After a month or so of stubbies, these long legs feel about as weird and alien to the amputee as a pair of stilts would feel to an able-bodied person.' The exact choice of artificial legs depends not just on the injuries to a soldier's real legs, but also on what other damage he's sustained. 'The more the patient's missing, the more complex it is. If they're a triple amputee then the whole process of putting those limbs on becomes much more complicated. If you've only got one hand, and that might be missing a finger, it's much, much more difficult.'

The most advanced legs are the Geniums, which at the time of writing cost around £30,000 – each – and have six separate sensors in the movable joints (ankle and knee) as well as gyroscopes, strain gauges, inclinometers, and systems to store and release energy. I examine a Genium: it's a work of art, and Mark knows exactly what I'm thinking.

'Makes you realise how amazing your own legs are, doesn't it?' he says.

The process of getting people walking again begins on two parallel bars set into the floor. They're only a few metres long, but for the soldier who's learning to walk again those few metres can seem like a marathon. Drenched in sweat, arm muscles quivering with the strain, their progress can be agonisingly slow.

One leg forward. Pause. Other leg forward. Pause. Repeat.

It's hard to get going and just as hard to stop: you have to shift your weight in much the same way as a skier does when executing a parallel turn.

Reach the end. Turn round. Do it again.

It's not always as simple as this, of course. Progress in many cases is zigzag rather than linear: a man might get so far and then have to go for another round of surgery, lose his momentum and have to start again. But these are soldiers, these are warriors – they don't give up.

Physical rehabilitation like this is the most obvious side of what Headley offers. You see it not just in the prosthetics department but also in the swimming pool and in any of the complex's three gyms – Waterloo, Trafalgar and Battle of Britain – where instructors work their patients on anti-gravity treadmills (which can be programmed to take all or some of the user's weight), circuit exercises, weights sessions or contact wheelchair sports. If you didn't look too closely, this could be any gym in the country: loud music, the steam-engine breathing of people working hard, the odd burst of laughter.

But physical rehab is not the only thing which Headley offers – far from it. The professionals here concentrate on the mind as much as the body. There are psychiatrists, psychologists and mental health nurses. Some patients need listening to as much as they need rebuilding. They have flashbacks, nightmares and feelings of guilt. Sometimes they talk to a counsellor, sometimes they just sit quietly with a nurse till they're settled again.

And sometimes – quite often, in fact – they find solace and comfort in one of Headley Court's most unique features: its garden.

A lot of blokes at Headley say the same kind of things when they're first offered horticultural therapy – 'No, not for me, thanks, mate', 'Bit boring, isn't it?' and even 'It's posh middle-aged women who do gardening, not my sort'. But often they don't get the option of saying no. Headley is a military establishment, and its patients are subject to military discipline when they're here: their duty is to work themselves to get better. Turning down a session because you think 'it's not for me' is no more acceptable than missing parade or disobeying orders.

And these rough, tough soldiers find a curious but profound peace in Headley's gardens. They're beautiful (the gardens, not the soldiers), but they also need maintenance, and the patients play a part in this just as much as the full-time professional groundsmen do.

It's only a few hundred metres from the M25, but the trees

muffle most of the traffic noise, and so the atmosphere is one of timeless stillness. In decades past men came back to places like this from Passchendaele and the Somme, from Flanders and Ypres, from El Alamein and Normandy.

They come here now too.

They dig and plant and weed and tend seeds and water and potter round the kitchen garden. In one corner is a small area called 'Thoughts of Home': a postage stamp, really, a small picket fence enclosing a wooden hut, a bughouse and some shrubs, but a place which draws these men like moths to a flame.

They lose themselves in the simple effort of the task at hand. Gardening is beneficial in many ways – it helps with balance, fine motor skills and confidence – but it also gives these men something more holistic: a connection to nature, the feeling of soil beneath their fingernails, the symphonies of birds overhead, the wind and rain and sun on their backs.

A tranquility. A healing. Nothing but them and the gardens. No IEDs, no insurgents, no threat, no danger … Just them and the gardens.

Many patients do several stints in Headley Court. On any admission subsequent to their first, they come to the gardens to see how the work they did last time is looking now. Some of them almost track or judge their own recovery depending on how the garden is.

'Dig for Victory', the World War Two slogan went. These men dig for victory too. Their triumphs are smaller and often unseen, but no less important for that.

Even on a cold March day, I feel as though I could stay forever in this bucolic, thoroughly English Eden. But of course I can't. More to the point, nor can they.

This is one of the paradoxes of Headley Court, and indeed of any rehabilitation centre worth the name: the better you make it, the more fulfilling and uplifting the experience, the less your patients want to leave. But leave they must.

They call it the 'Headley bubble', and it's amazing, but it's not real life. 'We don't do happy ever after,' says Lt Col Rhodri Phillip, Clinical Lead for Complex Trauma Rehabilitation. 'We do the maximum functional capacity that your injuries will allow.' All Headley's myriad programmes are designed not as ends in themselves but with real-world applications in mind.

Why do you need to be able to squat down and stand up again? So you can pick your child up off the floor.

Why do you need to be able to swim without legs? So you can go to the beach when you're on holiday.

That kind of thing. As normal a life as possible. So even while they're being treated at Headley, patients are encouraged to interact with the real world as much as possible. Staff will take a bunch of amputees on their artificial legs out

107

on excursions. Guildford High Street's a favourite, as it has steep cobbled sections and old worn steps without handrails. Or Brighton seafront, all packed with crowds. Maybe Chelsea Flower Show for the horticulturalists, because most people there are too busy gazing at the gardens to look where they're going, which in turn forces the amputees to be alert and take evasive action (or, as happened to one of them, to react with a smile when an old lady offered him her walking stick).

Escalators. Buses (especially going up to the top deck and down again). Rollercoasters and theme parks. Go into a shoe shop and ask for a pair of shoes, not least to see how you react to those reacting to you. If you can do all this then you should do all this, goes the thinking, and if you can't do all this then you should learn to.

Nor does Headley stop at these everyday requirements. Their aim is to allow people to continue in the services, but they also know that sometimes – as in Simi's case, for example – this just isn't possible. And preparing people for life outside the services is very different even from preparing them to carry on within the services in a different, less physically active role than before.

One of the central tenets of any armed force is that its members are special – that, simply through earning the right to wear the uniform, they're set apart from the civilian herd. When you wear that uniform you have to believe you're invincible, otherwise there's no point in you being there.

But when you're given a medical discharge, by definition you're no longer invincible. And those civilians you were told you were more special than? Well, you're now one of them. And those civilians have spent years knowing how Civvy Street works while you've been told where to be and what to do and when to eat and shit and shower and shave every minute of every day of your life in uniform, so you'd better start catching up fast.

That's why Headley organise job placements and work trials, house and vehicle adaptations. They offer life skills: financial advice, legal advice, insurance claims advice, advice on how to deal with dysfunctional families. 'The guys need this kind of stuff,' says Lt Col Phillip. 'A lot of people join the infantry because they have to, they're not giving up a City job to get there. And if you give them the tools then they'll respond. Life is 10 per cent what happens to you and 90 per cent how you respond to it. One of the guys who was here is now working as a gamekeeper, something he'd never have done otherwise. He's loving it. That's what I want. I'd rather have 20 gamekeepers than one gold medal at the Paralympics.'

A former patient wrote: 'Headley Court will always remain

lodged in my heart as a force for good: a bottomless well of determination, fortitude and courage that I can dip into when I feel the need. It put me back together physically, healed me mentally, and gave me a cast-iron belief in my own abilities.'

Headley Court is closing down in 2018: the facility is moving to a new purpose-built centre at Stanford Hall in Leicestershire. The amazing work done here will go on: it will just be in a different place, and it will continue to improve and change. So many extraordinary people have passed through these doors: so many triumphs, so many disasters, so many stories imprinted on the ground through those artificial legs and carried on the wind through the gardens.

On the way out, I see a photographic exhibition in the main hall. One of the pictures is a black-and-white shot of Group Captain Teresa Griffiths, Headley Court's commanding officer. Beneath the picture, she has written her own view of the place:

Headley Court is a place where:
Science meets magic.
Dreams can be transformed into reality.
Patients are central to everything we do.
Honesty and kindness matters.

Laughter is a medicine.

Hope and courage foster new beginnings.

Expectations are changed.

Small steps can change lives.

The definition of normal is challenged and redefined without boundaries.

Everyone cares.

Not every soldier is eligible to go to Headley. It's only for members of the British armed forces, for a start, although they do very occasionally take members of other nations' forces by special arrangement. But its spirit and its aims are shared by all those who strive to be part of the Invictus Games, no matter where they come from.

Josh Boggi did go to Headley after returning from Afghanistan. He learned to walk the same way as everyone else did there: held upright in sweat-soaked harnesses, inching along the parallel bars, that glorious first moment when he took his first steps unaided.

Now he was normal, more or less. He could stand upright to the same height he was before, though everyone tried to get an extra couple of inches when the Blatchford guys were measuring them for prosthetic legs, everyone gave it the 'Yeah, I was six foot three before', and the Blatchford guys just laughed because they'd heard it all before.

Being at Headley had its perks. For four years Josh been on the waiting list to go and see *Top Gear* being filmed. Now the producers were offering tickets to the guys at Headley. A split second standing on an IED had got him in quicker than four years of being able-bodied. Ah well, that's how it went. That was life. And Josh wanted more of it – 'I wanted to kick the arse out of life.'

In 2013 he saw someone riding a handbike – a recumbent tricycle low to the ground with two wheels at the back, a steerable wheel at the front and hand cranks providing the power through a standard derailleur gearing. He had a go himself. Six weeks later, he cycled from London to Paris as part of the Help for Heroes Big Battlefield Bike Ride. He was the first ever triple amputee to do it, which made him proud, but it was the collective effort which really moved him – 'Being part of a team was the best part. It replaces some of what you lose when you leave the Army, it was like coming off tour again.'

He thought the bike ride would be a one-off. For a while he just enjoyed himself – 'Too many beers, too much Domino's.' But he knew he needed something else to feed the craving.

It was March 2014. Prince Harry was on TV announcing that the first Invictus Games would be held in September, six months away. Josh looked at himself in the mirror.

'Right, you fat bastard,' he told his reflection. 'Time to get in shape.'

Where Josh Boggi had been given no option with his amputations, both Sarah Rudder and Mike Goody had actively chosen to have the chop. All surgery is inherently risky, no matter how remote that risk, and wilfully electing to have one of your limbs removed is something beyond the imagination of most people (there is a rare psychiatric disorder which causes otherwise healthy people to want to have limbs amputated, but that's an entirely different issue).

But when you're in such unrelenting agony, as both Sarah and Mike were, and when you so desperately want to be active again, the choice isn't really a choice.

For both of them, it was the best thing imaginable. 'If I'd known how much freedom it would give me,' Sarah said, 'I'd have done it sooner. I felt like I could challenge myself again.'

The surgeon pulled her muscles and tendons down and wrapped them around the back of her calf to provide more cushioning around the base of the stump. To start with, when she had some problems with the stump being sore and her prosthetic not fitting properly, 'there was a time where you feel like you're not going to be whole again because you're missing a piece,' but once she sorted out her prosthetic issues she quickly taught herself how to adapt.

Nor was she confined to doing things only when she was wearing it. She took up surfing at San Onofre State Beach, for example, with the left leg of her wetsuit neatly tied off beneath her knee. Paddle out, catch a wave, get up on her knees and ride the wave for a few seconds before falling over in gales of laughter – 'It was like flying.'

For Mike, the freedom of not having to rely on other people was the biggest immediate change – 'My confidence shot back up, and suddenly I was full of plans – go back to university, be a paramedic, those kind of things.' Of course there were sceptics who saw only his artificial leg and not the man above it, but he didn't care: 'Being told I can't do something just motivates me. Because of what happened I no longer think, "I'll do that tomorrow," as there might not be a tomorrow. I've got to do what I want to do now.'

There were people who thought he wouldn't be able to run a 10K race. He ran one. There were those who told him he wouldn't be able to work for the Ambulance Service. He proved them wrong too, getting a job with the South East Coast Ambulance Service. 'Once I was carrying an old lady down the stairs to the ambulance, and she suddenly remembered I only had one leg and started freaking out. But I just laughed and said, "I've carried plenty of heavier people than you, love."'

He narrowly missed out on selection for the Walking with the Wounded race to the South Pole in 2013, where three teams of wounded servicemen and women (one team from the UK, one from the US and the third from Australia and Canada combined) raced on foot across 335 Antarctic kilometres in temperatures of −35°C.

All these things that Sarah and Mike couldn't do with two legs, they suddenly found they could do with one. So of course they decided to mark their new-found freedom in their own way.

Sarah decorated her sprinting prosthetic with a picture of Wonder Woman.

Mike got a tattoo on the calf of his other leg. It said simply: 'I miss my friend.'

As Sarah and Mike's lives became more active, so they found it easier to keep their post-traumatic stress symptoms manageable, if not completely at bay. Stephan Moreau and Darlene Brown have found the same thing.

The Chemox incident which triggered Stephan's symptoms was classified as an operational stress injury. For a while, he thought that he didn't really deserve comparison with someone who had a 'proper' injury: someone who'd stood on an IED in Afghanistan, for example: 'I was telling myself that my injury was not as severe as theirs, and I was a bit ashamed to share it. But once I did start to share, I realised trauma is trauma. People react differently and we all get affected differently. I had to stop comparing.'

As well as regular counselling sessions, he began training – 'When I went out for a nice run, or bike ride or swim, I felt so much better. Not just physically but mentally. It took the pressure off. It decompressed me, made me physically exhausted. I was too tired to be stressed, it helped a lot.'

He set his sights on doing triathlons: not just any old triathlon, either, but an Ironman. A three-course meal of pure pain: a 2.4-mile swim to start with, a main course of 112 miles on the bike and then a marathon for dessert. That stubbornness, that self-reliance, saw him through it.

He also found that, like the Navy, triathlon has its own community. The triathlon forums he'd surfed while in the grip of drinking too much he now returned to, clear-eyed and ready to share what he'd gone through – 'I was open about my addictions. I was contacted by a few people who were struggling and I was able to share my experience with recovery and helped them out. There are so many people, good people, out there. It's amazing.'

As for Darlene, that 15-mile drive from her home to the Mates4Mates headquarters was the hardest thing she'd ever done. It was also the best thing she'd ever done. 'That first drive is massive,' said Janice Johnston, who was assigned to be Darlene's psychologist. 'It's taking a step toward recovery, it's choosing not to stay at home.'

Darlene took a 12-week course under the tutelage of Dr Andrew Khoo, one of Australia's leading PTSD specialists. He was adamant right from the start that her condition was treatable: 'If you define cure as removing symptoms and getting people back to functioning fully then, yes, there is a cure.'

But as with Stephan Moreau, it was physical activity which did as much for Darlene's recovery as anything else. Mates4Mates were sending some guys to Europe for the Big Battlefield Bike Ride – the same event in which Josh Boggi had become the first ever triple-amputee participant – and they asked Darlene whether she wanted to come too. She hadn't been on a bike in God knows how long. And only a short time before, even 15 miles across Brisbane, had seemed like a trip across galaxies, so the idea of a 24-hour flight to the other side of the world was clearly ludicrous.

She said yes, she'd love to go.

It was hard, the ride. Physically hard, just to do the distance. Socially hard, to be in such a big group when she'd been used to being on her own for so long. And mentally hard too, navigating traffic coming at her from the wrong direction and driven by lunatic Frenchmen rather than the more sedate Australian drivers back home.

But she kept at it. And somewhere on those backroads of northern France, wheat fields one side and old Gaston put-put-putting in his ancient 2CV the other, she felt her mind being cleansed. The effort, the regularity, the wind, the pace, the peace ... it was all balm to her troubled soul.

She didn't have to be the best at anything: she was giving it a go, and that in itself made her happy. Soon she found herself laughing and joking with people on the bike and again in the evenings at the hotels. One night, she saw someone she hadn't seen for 15 years.

Herself.

The old Darlene was back.

Exercise was proving Bart Couprie's salvation too. In normal circumstances he hated it, but now it gave him a sense of purpose. It went some way towards taking off the weight he'd put on and restoring the muscle mass he'd lost, and most of all it seemed to be more or less keeping the depression at bay.

With exercise came the urge to proselytise. He thought of the Navy's core values: courage, comradeship and commitment. He could keep quiet about what he was suffering – it was pretty embarrassing, after all – or he could bite the bullet and try to get the word out. It would take courage, sure. But . it would show comradeship to others who might be in the same position, and it would show commitment to actually trying to make things better for people.

He thought of a story he'd heard about a Maori man – 'He'd gone to the doctor, complaining about a problem in the water works. When the doctor stuck his finger up the bloke's bum, he was so shocked that he pulled up his pants, left the surgery and never went back. The prostate cancer killed him, but actually what he died of was embarrassment.'

Bart began to spread the word. He didn't worry if it made him look personally foolish, as long as it did some good for other people. He called his twin brother, Boudewijn, and told him to get himself checked out. Boudewijn had no symptoms, but it turned out he had early-stage prostate cancer too: so early, in fact, that it was easily cured with surgical removal.

One good deed ticked off, many more to go.

Bart climbed Auckland's Sky Tower in full firefighting gear for charity and told his story to TV shows and magazines. He dealt with people's discomfort head-on: 'I can guarantee you there are quite a few men out there who can't get over the fact that I've had fingers and implements shoved up my bum and are wondering how I can talk about it so openly. Well, it's blindingly simple: undiagnosed prostate cancer is a lot worse for you than the temporary insertion of fingers and implements. People have got to, excuse the pun, take their head out of their arse about this.'

The more he talked about it, the more he felt comfortable talking about it. The aggressive treatment of his own cancer was paying dividends too. His PSA began to fall and his odds of full remission began to rise: 'Looks like touch wood, I'll come back to normal, or as normal as I've ever been. You see, a funny thing happened on my way to misery: I never got there. I am instead, honestly, openly and exceedingly happy.'

Mary Wilson was happy too. On an August day in 2014, she reached the summit of An Gearanach. It was both just another one of the 282 Munros and yet a special one too: for it was the 282nd one she'd climbed.

She'd done it.

After leaving the Army she worried that her focus, determination and commitment might all tail off, but this was as hard a physical feat as she'd ever managed. Sometimes she'd had to cross rivers which ran waist-high around her. Sometimes she'd pushed on through snow and hail (it was Scotland, after all, where there are only two seasons, winter and bad weather). Sometimes she'd had to use technical climbing and abseiling skills which, with her MS, had pushed her to the limits. And always she'd needed her partner Judi

Maurice Manuel (black jersey #9) during tip-off at the Danish National Championship.

Maurice Manuel during his fifth deployment. Photo taken after one of many patrols in Rahim Kalay in Helmand, Afghanistan in 2008.

Josh Boggi and his partner Anna at the Invictus Games Orlando 2016.

Sarah Rudder, USMC vet. 'You never know how strong you are until being strong is your only choice' (Bob Marley).

Sarah Rudder with her seven medals from the Invictus Games Orlando 2016.

Stephan Moreau competing in indoor rowing at the Invictus Games Orlando 2016.

Mike Goody with his partner Sara at the Invictus Games Orlando 2016.

Maurillia Simpson living her childhood dream as a soldier.

Darlene Brown with friend and fellow Team Australia competitor Mark Urquhart at the Invictus Games Orlando 2016.

A 21-year-old Bart Couprie (2nd left) with his twin brother Boudewyn, and Ron and Roger Sheehan. Taken while deployed in Sembawang, Singapore in 1988.

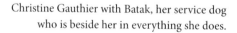

Christine Gauthier with Batak, her service dog who is beside her in everything she does.

Mary Wilson
during one of her
swimming training
sessions.

Phillip Thompson (2nd left) at the Invictus
Games London 2014.

Phillip Thompson in Afghanistan talking with
the villagers' children. This was the day before
Phil was critically wounded by an improvised
explosive device.

Sébastien David at the Invictus Games Orlando 2016 with his family: wife Nathalie, son Axel and daughter Lucie.

Zoe Williams, second from right, with fellow UK team competitors at the Invictus Games Orlando 2016 Closing Ceremony.

Fabio Tomasulo with his fellow Italian team competitors at the Invictus Games Orlando 2016.

Amy Baynes took up archery for the 2014 Invictus Games as a way to challenge herself with a sport she'd never thought of doing.

Kai Cziesla taking part in the Crossfit Open 2017.

'I won the silver medal in Orlando in the 4-minute indoor-rowing competition. This is why I had tattooed the medal on my wounded leg.'

Rahmon Zondervan in Afghanistan, two weeks before he was wounded by an IED explosion.

to guide her, as she could no longer orientate a map or read a compass properly.

She'd done it.

'I felt really emotional about climbing the last one. It was something I had strived for that I never believed I'd reach.'

The metaphor, of course, was not lost on her: the actual mountains she'd climbed were a reflection of all the hurdles she'd had to overcome ever since the drunkard in Hong Kong had attacked her, 20 years before.

Maurillia Simpson was also overcoming her hurdles. The man phoning her was someone who'd met her at a Forces networking event. He'd remembered her name and her enthusiasm, despite the trials she'd been through. He was in charge of providing security for the Olympic Park and Westfield Stratford City. Was she interested in coming to talk to him about a job?

She certainly was. And after so long with the odds stacked against her, the wheel of fortune finally seemed to be turning her way. Not only did she get the job, but her new boss then got onto a housing association and petitioned them to give Simi priority for an adapted flat.

'I consider myself almost freakishly lucky to have ended up where I am,' she says now. 'I'm in the former Olympic athletes' village. When I need to train, I make the short trip over to Queen Elizabeth Park, where my job is. When I open the curtains in the morning and look across London, my first thought is breakfast, not finding a place to crash. I've been able to imagine a new dream.' But she knows it was close. 'I've heard of many veterans that have fallen by the wayside – I could have been one of them.'

Simi takes part in several different sports, including shot-put, discus and sitting volleyball. But sports is not all she's done outside work. The Welsh poet Owen Sheers wrote a play called *The Two Worlds of Charlie F*, a collection of military testimonials, and wanted soldiers rather than professional actors to perform it. The producer, Alice Driver, had been inspired by a friend injured in Afghanistan, who'd explained to her that when a soldier's badly injured, 'You lose your sense of self-worth, your dignity, your personality and what you always wanted to be.'

Simi couldn't have put it better herself. Alice, who had auditioned service personnel through the Royal British Legion, asked her whether she wanted to be part of it. Simi didn't have to ask twice.

'It gave me an adopted family,' Simi says. 'I had brothers, and not just brothers in arms. I had friends made in a different sort of battle. We were all dealing with our injuries, our bad days, good days and not-so-good days. It gave me a sense of belonging to a team again, something I thought I'd lost when I lost my dream.'

The play is an ensemble piece, presented in a number of different ways: video clips, choreography, statements, communal briefings, enacted flashbacks and so on. Yet the most powerful section of all, the one which so many audience members said made the hairs on their neck stand up, the 'wow' moment, was Simi's and hers alone.

Just before the interval she stepped to the front of stage and, her voice rising and falling with nothing but her own skill and emotion for company, she sang to the audience the same song she'd sung to herself while trapped beneath the wall in Basra.

Why should I feel discouraged, why should the shadows
  come,
Why should my heart be lonely, and long for heav'n and
  home,
When Jesus is my portion? My constant friend is He:
His eye is on the sparrow, and I know He watches me;
His eye is on the sparrow, and I know He watches me.

I sing because I'm happy, I sing because I'm free,
For His eye is on the sparrow, and I know He watches me.
'Let not your heart be troubled,' His tender word I hear,

UNCONQUERABLE

And resting on His goodness, I lose my doubts and fears;
Though by the path He leadeth, but one step I may see;
His eye is on the sparrow, and I know He watches me;
His eye is on the sparrow, and I know He watches me.

Whenever I am tempted, whenever clouds arise,
When songs give place to sighing, when hope within me
    dies,
I draw the closer to Him, from care He sets me free;
His eye is on the sparrow, and I know He watches me;
His eye is on the sparrow, and I know He watches me.

PHIL THOMPSON, AUSTRALIA

When Phil Thompson says he only remembers bits and pieces, it's neither a figure of speech nor a way of getting out of answering awkward questions. He only remembers bits and pieces of his childhood: 'I have little bits of memory – what primary school I went to, what high school I went to – but not much.' He only remembers bits and pieces of joining the Army, aged 17, and being posted to East Timor for six months with Charlie Company 9 Platoon. He only remembers bits and pieces of doing reconnaissance training and being sent to Afghanistan in 2009. He only remembers bits and pieces of his time in Afghanistan, though enough to know it was the best time of his life. And he only remembers bits and pieces of the IED which exploded a metre from him one day on patrol in Uruzgan.

'I remember a dust cloud and the medic running in, pulling me out and checking me over. I don't really remember much after that. I had stuff on my sunglasses, like little pebbles, so I couldn't see out of them. I remember a ringing in my head, but that could just be – that's always there so it could just be me thinking that. But I don't remember much. Just a big dust plume, and the medic running in to help me.'

The reason he only remembers bits and pieces of all these things is that the blast left him with traumatic brain injury, as well as hearing loss, tinnitus, PTSD and depression – 'I battled with the rollercoaster of mental health for quite a while, even trying to take my own life.' He was given a medical discharge in 2011, and soon after – still carrying around a booklet reminding him what he had to do each day – he decided that this could go one of two ways: he could either wallow in what had happened, or he could use the experience to try and help others.

He chose the latter.

The Returned and Services League of Australia (RSL), which supports veterans, offered him a job as pensions and welfare officer – 'The role kind of puts you in the space of helping. It opens your mind a little to what actually happens: what legislation people are under, the hoops people have to jump through, and I think it's important that people know and understand that. Because when you're in a fragile state, you want things done yesterday and that can become a key stressor. And then things can become bad; they're not, but in a vet's mind they are.'

Since then he's moved and expanded roles across several different organisations, including the Australian federal government, but always with the aim of supporting veterans. He helps former servicemen and women find meaningful employment when they need it, and runs a peer support programme, where 'we take someone who's tracking relatively OK, and someone who's maybe not tracking so well, and we pair them together, supported by psychologists. It's non-rank focused and non-clinical:

it gives them someone to talk to, like a buddy system. Talking to someone who understands us, like someone you're paired with, that can help.'

He's quick to point out that helping other people is not just altruistic, he gets the benefits as much as they do: 'My mental health's been up and down, quite fluid, but I'm usually in a good place because helping people puts me in a good space. It's always very rewarding to see that I can help others who may have gone through a similar experience to me. I've been through some very difficult and dark times but I've managed to come out of it. I think because I can speak from a true-life experience, people tend to trust me and listen to me. If I can save someone's life and show them that there's life after injury, that's all I can ask for.'

One of Phil's favourite methods of empowering the vets he works with is sport. He helps organise sporting tournaments for Australian veterans at five separate levels of competition – local, regional, state, national and international. 'Sport's so amazing. There is no wrong door. There is no injury you can come to me with that I can't find something for you. People always say, "RSLs, they're just about beers, pokies and parmys [chicken parmigiana]" which, yeah, everyone likes. But for people between the ages of 17 and say 40, they want to be out playing sport, getting active. Coming in with sport, you're going to open the doors to the younger generations being involved. It's not enough to say you're wounded or injured, I won't accept it. If I tell another wounded person that they can do it, it resonates much better than coming from someone who isn't wounded, injured or ill. We're not defined by our injuries, we're defined by our actions.'

He pauses. 'That said, if you're an arsehole, you're an arsehole.'

The question of sport brings him to the Invictus Games. Phil competed in the first Games in London: 'More than just competing, it was the camaraderie which I loved. My sport was powerlifting, but as I was new to it, I don't think I was as prepared as I should have been. But I was so lucky because the British Armed Forces team really helped me out. Their coach, Ben Richens, gave me some advice and allowed me to train with his team. Otherwise I wouldn't have known any of the rules. I was now an "honorary Brit". I got tips from the likes of Micky Yule [who lost both legs in Afghanistan and came fourth in the parasport powerlifting at the 2014 Commonwealth Games] and I made some lifelong mates. To me this is what the Invictus Games ethos is all about: countries helping each other in sport as we did on the battlefield. We weren't so much competing against each other as feeling like fighting overseas, one team, all brothers and sisters. Plus, let's be honest, I raised the standard of humour and looks the Brits were obviously lacking in!'

For the 2016 Orlando Games he doubled up as both competitor and coach, helping out with both the powerlifters and the wheelchair rugby team: 'It was important to show that these things have a lifecycle. You compete, then you become a coach with what you've learned from competing, then maybe you become a team manager with what you've learned from both competing and coaching. You do your bit and then you move on so someone else can have the opportunities you had. It's irresponsible to give selection to the same guys again and again. And it's a challenge for you too. You become a manager, you have to think about a whole bunch of things – athletes, logistics, families, operational stuff – which you never had to worry about before. You can't just sit in one spot, you need to create and be involved in all different levels, otherwise you won't develop.'

He loved pretty much everything about both his Invictus Games experiences – 'You get treated like celebrities. There are cameras, there are paparazzi, there's royalty. But you need to be prepared, because it can be overwhelming. All that attention, not to mention the extent of some people's injuries – in London the British and Americans had more amputee competitors than we had team members full stop – if you're not careful it can debilitate rather than inspire you.'

Phil was awarded the RSL's 2016 ANZAC of the Year Award in recognition of his commitment to helping younger veterans. The fact that any ANZAC Award by definition spans the Tasman Sea amuses him: 'New Zealand? Isn't that like another Australian state or something? Do you even need your passport?'

Whichever capacity he occupies for the Australian team in Toronto, you suspect he'll be the target for some good-natured abuse from his Kiwi mates. And that, you also suspect, is just how he likes it.

4

HOW CHARGED WITH PUNISHMENTS THE SCROLL

Marriage is tough; marriage in the military is 10 times tougher. When a service member enlists, so does their family. Being a military spouse – and nine times out of 10 that means being a military wife – can sometimes feel like you get all the downsides of forces' life and precious few of the upsides.

The man you love is out in a war zone, but he has his mates around him and he's doing what he was trained to do. You, on the other hand, have no control and all the worry: that low-level, nagging itch that one morning the doorbell will ring and there'll be two men in uniform standing on the doorstep, and just from the look on their faces you'll know how bad it is before they've even said a word.

Want to talk to your husband on deployment? You can't: at least, you can't when you want to, only when he's able to spare the time and get a connection. Even then, it'll only be for a couple of minutes at a time, no more. No Skype, no FaceTime. You can't ask him how his day is or what he's doing, or where he is or when he's coming back, because he's not allowed to tell you any of that. You can't tell him about anything bad at home because you don't want to stress him out when there's nothing he can do about it. You can tell him that you love him and you miss him, but he already knows that. You hope.

What do you miss? People always ask you this and they always smirk when they do, expecting the obvious answer. But that's not what you miss most. What you miss most is just having him around, those little moments of connection between husband and wife: sitting on the sofa, laughing together at some cheesy sitcom on TV, standing unseen in the doorway as he reads the kids a bedtime story and they look up at him with wide eyes full of endless love, the cup of tea he brings you first thing every morning.

When he's off on deployment, the house feels very still. You can hear everything, even the smallest sounds, the ones you don't notice when he's there: the swirl of the wine as you pour yourself a glass, the children shifting in their sleep upstairs, the thoughts and worries chasing themselves round and round your head.

So you keep yourself busy because otherwise you'll go mad. Work can eat up lots of hours, family much more.

You're basically a single parent, so you have to be both Mum and Dad and do everything: cooking, washing, ironing, school runs, changing nappies, walking the dog, putting the rubbish out, getting the car fixed, organising birthday parties, dealing with teachers and bank managers, calling the plumber or the electrician, doing the tax returns, paying the bills. Everything. Even lawyers, because when your husband's in the military then things like wills and funeral plans and widow's pensions aren't just abstract and remote, they're there for a reason.

And when you do everything, that leaves no space for someone else. He comes back from deployment – the exact time of arrival will change at least three times beforehand – and there are the tearful reunions on parade grounds or docksides which the TV cameras capture, but once the front door's shut behind you it's not easy just to slot back into how things were before. It's not starting again from scratch, of course, but sometimes it feels not far off that. The kids have changed, he's changed, you've changed. Your lives are moving on, but sometimes in parallel and sometimes not, and that's hard.

Then there's all the actual moving. Go here. Go there. Go some place else. Once every two or three years is pretty standard. Once a year isn't unusual. Sometimes you get a nice place on a good base, sometimes you don't, but either way it's not your home, not really. It's not somewhere you get to put down roots. You watch how your kids adapt to this nomadic life, and part of you is proud that they get to be so good at making friends so quickly, and another part of you can't bear the flipside, that they also get to be good at saying goodbye without a backward glance.

'Ah well,' people say, 'you chose this life.'

No, you didn't: you chose your husband and the life came with it.

There are lots of positives too, of course. A ready-made community wherever you go, a genuine sense of pride in helping someone serve his country. And there are moments which will live with you forever: a ship pulling into harbour after months at sea, a military wedding with everyone in their dress uniform, a change of command ceremony executed with such exquisite timing it looks like ballet.

But in general it's hard. Harder than 'normal' life, civilian life. But not half as hard as it is when you send someone off and get them back not still whole but in pieces.

Sara Trott met Mike Goody just before the first Invictus Games in 2014. 'That was his chat-up line,' she says. '"Do you want to come and watch me competing at the Invictus Games?" Not a bad line.'

'And it worked,' Mike reminds her with a laugh.

His physical injuries were obvious to her right from the start, of course, but it wasn't long before she began to glimpse the mental scars too. Sara works for a company which pairs service dogs with people who need them – much like the organisation in Canada which had provided Christine Gauthier with Batak – so she was used to seeing people who were facing more than their fair share of troubles, but dealing with the symptoms of Mike's PTSD was something else entirely.

It was the friends and families of other Invictus Games competitors who got her through it.

'Invictus goes really big on families and friends,' she says. 'They know that behind every competitor are people without whom that competitor wouldn't be here, and they want to show their appreciation for that.' You stay in the same hotels, you take the same buses to and from the venues, you all sit together when you watch, so you get to know the other halves in the same way the competitors know each other.

'It's a cliché, but the military really is a big family. We all connected on social media. The banter aside, they've been amazing when I needed help. The first few times I saw Mike's post-traumatic stress symptoms, I didn't really know what to do. Why was he shutting me out? Was it something I'd done? Was it personal? So I sent messages saying "Help! What do

I do?" And they'd all write back saying no, no, it's not you. We've all been through it, here's how we cope with it.'

Dealing with a partner who has post-traumatic stress can be as hard as dealing with the stress itself. As an anonymous Australian veteran said of his wife: 'I've put her through hell, absolute hell. I feel horrible for doing it. You don't mean to. You indirectly take it out on them, your family, your children. And you know that all they want to do is help, but it just seems like there's nothing they can do sometimes and sometimes you think that they'd be better without you.'

Through the support of the other wives and girlfriends Sara found various coping strategies: 'The anniversary is always bad for Mike – in fact, there are two anniversaries, the explosion and the amputation – so on those days every year we go and do something fun. Go to Alton Towers, go away for a couple of days.'

Even simple things like that can greatly help when dealing with post-traumatic stress sufferers. Steer them away from triggers as much as possible. Agree time-outs when arguments become too heated to allow the sufferer to calm themselves down. Don't walk on eggshells or avoid the issue, but don't force things when it's clear they're feeling vulnerable.

'I know now when to be sympathetic and when to say, "Put your leg on and get me a drink,"' Sara says.

Her support of Mike is mirrored again and again across the kaleidoscope of Invictus Games competitors. Mary Wilson knows how much she owes to her partner, Judi, an Alzheimer's researcher. Bart Couprie has had Jude standing by him every step of his battle against prostate cancer. Sarah Rudder's husband has been with her on her long journey back from the flames of the Pentagon. So too Darlene Brown's husband on her return from internal exile. Josh Boggi calls his partner Anna, 'My rock. I try and do everything myself, but if I can't, I know I've got someone there who will help me and always be there.'

All these people reflect one of humanity's fundamental truths: that the basic unit for love and survival is not one but two. In varying degrees they've had to deal with their partners' physical limitations, anger, depression, self-blame, guilt, adjustment difficulties and a hundred other things. They've had to do this while balancing their needs with their own, and sometimes with those of their children too. The road to recovery is one they take together. You can't fix a family while an individual is broken, nor can you fix an individual while a family is broken: you are damaged together and you heal together.

Nor is it just families on whom the competitors rely: it's their friends too. And sometimes it's a stranger who comes across them by complete chance and ends up becoming as inseparable a part of their lives as they do of hers.

Kath Ryan had no connection with the military other than the one most Britons have: ancestors who fought under conscription in the two World Wars. Her grandfather had seen action in World War One; a quarter of a century later, her uncle had been part of the ground crew for the RAF's 617 Squadron, better known as the Dam Busters. But other than that, nothing. Certainly nothing which would hint at what was to come.

Kath was a ward sister at Queen Elizabeth Hospital in Birmingham, but from 1991 onwards, she found it increasingly difficult to work after rupturing a disc in her back while moving a 27-stone patient on her own. She was forced into early retirement on health grounds, but many years later found herself back on site, more or less – in Selly Oak Hospital, right next door to QEH. Kath's sister Marie was recovering from a stroke, and Kath brought her some butterfly cakes when she went to visit.

A day or so later, Marie rang and asked for some more cakes.

'You *can't* have eaten them all already!' Kath said.

'I haven't.'

'Then who has?'

'The squaddies.'

Selly Oak was the first port of call for injured soldiers being flown back from Afghanistan, where the campaign was at its height. Marie had gone outside for some fresh air – well, to the smoking hut – with her cargo of Kath's butterfly cakes, and a posse of ravenous soldiers who for months had eaten nothing but army rations and hospital food had descended on her as though it were feeding time at the zoo.

'OK,' Kath said. 'I'll make you some more.'

'Er ... the squaddies ask, very nicely, if you could make them some too.'

'Sure. How many of them are there?'

'About 35.'

'*What?*'

Marie laughed. 'About 35. They're all lovely, and they're all hungry.'

Kath had loved baking for as long as she could remember. Her mother and grandmother had taught her, and for her baking meant happy memories and comfort. If she could give a little comfort to some guys who were obviously going through hard times, she'd do so with pleasure.

The next week, Kath went back with enough cakes for close on three dozen soldiers. She handed them out with smiles, and they all thanked her. That was her good deed for the day done. But when she got home, she was still thinking about those boys she'd seen – and they *were* boys, some of them, so pale and skinny now they weren't in uniform, missing arms and legs when they looked barely old enough to be shaving.

It was the first time she'd seen people with such injuries close up. Everyone knew the war in Afghanistan was going on, of course, and most people had some vague idea that conditions were punishing and that the soldiers out there were doing some pretty brave things, but the reality of it, young lads with wide eyes now facing a life very different than the one they'd hoped for – no, she hadn't really seen that before. The images kept playing in her mind. She thought about the way they bantered with each other, and the cheekiness which she knew masked deeper reserves of courage.

She wanted to do more for those boys. A few days later, she phoned Selly Oak and asked – even as she was speaking she found herself willing the nurse to give the answer she wanted to hear – asked whether the lads would like some more cake.

The nurse burst out laughing. 'Would they *ever*! I'll tell you, all we've heard since you left is, "Do you think she'll come back? Do you think she'll come back?"'

And that's how it started.

Every Wednesday, Kath would load up her car with cakes and drive the short distance from her house to Selly Oak.

There, she'd arrange the cakes and Tupperware containers on a hostess trolley, balancing them precariously as she had so many, and wheel the trolley round the ward. 'At every bed I'd stop and ask the occupant: "Can I lead you into temptation?" "What's on offer?" they'd reply. "Whatever's on the trolley, as long as it's legal or moral," I'd say. And off we'd go.'

She made as many different types of cake as was feasible, knowing not everyone liked the same things. A weekly bake might include six dozen butterflies, 10 banoffee pies, 48 vanilla slices, 24 carrot cakes and a tray of custard pies. Some asked for Rocky Road, others for Rice Krispies with white chocolate. For those men coming out of operations and not yet back on solids, she'd make shakes rather than cakes.

The soldiers started sending her letters. One (clearly a frustrated *Great British Bake Off* judge) wrote: 'I personally consider myself something of a cakey aficionado. I found the Victoria sponge to be truly magnificent, the sponge itself was deliciously light but still had substance and that most essential quality of moistness.' Another said: 'These are the best vanilla slices I have ever tasted. Worth being shot for!' A third credited her with single-handedly lowering the fatality rate – 'We're all too busy trying to stay alive another week so we can have some more cake' – and gave her what any

Briton will recognise as the ultimate compliment: 'You bake better than my nan.'

Kath found herself spending longer and longer there each week as she got to know the boys better and talked more deeply with them. There was a constant flow in and out of the wards – people being discharged or sent on to Headley Court, new injuries coming in on the transport planes from Kandahar and Bastion – but whoever they were, they looked forward to Kath's visits. Her fame had spread beyond the walls of Selly Oak: one bloke who arrived from Afghanistan told her that when he'd been shot, the first thing one of his mates had said was 'You lucky bastard, now you're going to get cake.'

When it was their birthday she'd make them birthday cakes with candles and balloons. At Christmas she'd dress up as Mother Christmas – 'Just to keep them up and let them know that people cared about them.' Soon she was churning out 500 portions a week and getting up at 3 a.m. to give herself enough time to do it.

It wasn't just cakes she was providing: it was love, it was laughter, it was someone who'd listen to them pour their hearts out or just sit in silence with them if they wanted. And the best thing about all this was that it was always organic, never forced. She hadn't sought them out or vice versa, it had just happened. That was what made it work, and that was what made it special. Everyone else with whom the soldiers came into contact wanted or needed something from them: doctors with their charts, commanding officers with their service schedules, families with all their hopes and fears.

Kath had none of that; she never judged, never pushed. On every visit she'd give each man three hugs: the first for all the guys she'd looked after up to that point, the second for the man himself and the third for all the guys yet to come. Often she'd meet the patients' families, so she made sure to bake enough for them too, knowing that the families are injured just as much as the soldiers themselves. She noted how wives and mothers would react differently to the sight of the man they loved missing a limb or more: 'The wives are all "Thank God he's alive". The mums are "My little boy's in bits".'

Sometimes she feared the worst, such as the day she went into a ward to see an empty bed, which the week before had contained an injured soldier. He'd seemed OK the last time she'd seen him, but she was a nurse and she knew how quickly conditions could deteriorate even when you didn't expect them to. IED blasts could easily cause secondary infections. Had he been carted off to intensive care? Or, God forbid …

'It's all right, love,' came a shout from the other side of the ward. 'He's down the pub.'

Then there was the young lad who never seemed to have any family around. Lots of other blokes would have wives and kids and parents and all sorts around his bed, but the youngster never had anybody. It was bad enough to have been blown up in Helmand, but then to come home and find yourself alone: well, Kath could hardly imagine. She didn't want to pry – she always let them tell her things at their own pace – but she also wanted to know if there was anything she could do to help. He might be an orphan or a foster kid. So she asked him. 'Oh no,' he said. 'My folks are up here the whole time but I tell them to clear off on Wednesdays so I can have you to myself.'

Kath saw the boys all the way through from admission to discharge, and often beyond: as well as her weekly trips to Selly Oak (and then QEH when Selly Oak closed), she'd also go to Headley once a month. For seven years she never took a holiday of more than five days: she'd see her boys on a Wednesday, go away Thursday through Monday, and be back Tuesday to bake all day for Wednesday in the hospital. It's for the same reason that she's never even applied to be a *Bake Off* contestant despite almost everyone she meets telling her that she should – 'I just don't have the time.'

It's taken over her life. To many people she's not Kath Ryan but Kath the Cake Lady. She burned through pretty much all her savings – and 10 separate ovens – before she set up as a charity, Cakes4Casualties, and began to receive donations. But she's also the first to say that she's got as much out of it as the boys have: 'It's such a privilege and a joy to be doing this for them. They've been my recovery as much as I've been theirs. I didn't do it to get anything back. From minute one when I walked in there I felt like I belonged. They've enriched life beyond my dreams. Their friendships mean so much to me. Every day, literally every day, I'll get an e-mail or a Facebook message from one of them. Five of them have invited me to their weddings this year alone.'

Her flat is full of display cases stuffed with badges and pins from all round the world, given to her by the men and women she's met. The names and colours jostle with each other for your attention: New Zealand Army, Airborne Forever, France, ex-WRAF on Tour, Fisher House, Wounded Warrior, Hasler Company. Wristbands are piled in neat pyramids: the Royal Welsh, the Royal Scots, Household Cavalry, Bomb Disposal. There are shoulder patches and teddy bears, polo shirts and T-shirts.

She shows me a T-shirt in the distinctive maroon of the Parachute Regiment. 'GOD IS AIRBORNE' it says on the front, with the Para crest above the word 'airborne'. 'Turn it over,' says Kath. On the back is the Royal Marines crest and the words 'HE FAILED THE COMMANDO COURSE'. She laughs. 'That's what they're all like, always chirping away at each other.'

It's not just soldiers whose lives she's helped, either. The photographer Giles Duley lost both legs and an arm after stepping on an IED – 'I was in many ways a broken man. My body had given every ounce of energy and my mind was struggling to deal with the new reality of being a triple amputee. It was an incredibly dark time. Kath's weekly visits were a huge lift. Her arrival would light up the ward, filling everyone with rare laughter and her unconditional kindness and love served as a reminder of home and future lives. I can't say how much her company and cakes meant to me. She really was a beacon of light during my darkest moment. I'm proud to call her a friend.'

She was in the crowd at the first Invictus Games in London: 'I'd seen these guys at their worst when they came back from Afghan, lost a lot of weight and were at the very beginning of their recovery path, and now I got to see them competing at a top world sporting event. It was just so amazing.'

But there seemed no way she could get to Orlando two years later – no way, that was, until one of the British competitors offered her a ticket as part of his family pass. It wouldn't be a proper British team without their Cake Lady, would it?

'It's only right that someone so instrumental to our recovery should be here with us for the Games,' said 2014 British team captain Dave Henson.

They even gave Kath her own escort – the Royal Marines Cake Lady Protection Unit. Only the elite need apply for selection, naturally. And only at the Invictus Games could this happen.

ZOE WILLIAMS, UNITED KINGDOM

Zoe Williams had a dream. It wasn't a dream she liked to articulate out loud, because even if everything went to plan it was still decades away, but it was something she aspired to deep within her. In almost 500 years of existence, the Royal Navy had never made a woman admiral: Zoe wanted to be the first.

'I grew up in Portsmouth, but we weren't a naval family: my dad was a GP. Then one day, aged 13, I went on a ship for a day and I was hooked, just hooked. I knew this was what I wanted to do with my life.' She joined up, aged 19, as a Warfare Officer, responsible for safe navigation and operation while at sea. When it came to the type of vessel she was on, you name it and she did it: patrol vessels, mine hunters, amphibious assault ships, time up at the nuclear submarine base at Faslane, near Glasgow. She loved it all and was good at it.

There was only one cloud on the horizon: 'I started getting lower leg pain and within two years my back was regularly aching. At first I thought it was just my body taking the toll from training sessions, and that it would pass. But over time it got worse and on one trip, after being at sea for just a few weeks, I was sent home. I had a bulge on one of the discs in my lower back.' The specialists told her that her condition might deteriorate

147

to the extent that she needed spinal surgery within 24 hours. Maritime deployments several months long and the possibility of urgent spinal surgery clearly didn't mix: one was going to have to give.

Zoe was taken off active duty and given a desk job, helping the long and complicated process of transferring the ownership of certain sites from the Ministry of Defence to the Royal Navy – 'Actually, it was fascinating. It gave me a real exposure to the business side of all that kind of thing, which I knew would stand me in good stead.'

But desk jobs do not admirals make – 'I knew that being in the Navy without ever being able to go to sea wasn't going to work, not long-term. I felt it was better to get out altogether than do it half-arsed.' She was the same age as all her friends leaving university, though they had degrees and she didn't. More to the point, they hadn't been forced to give up their dreams in the way she had.

Zoe was at a low ebb and didn't know how to haul herself out of it. Nor did she much care. Painkillers and fast food had replaced exercise and positivity – and she'd always been a positive person, so this slump was really out of character. The lazier she became, the lazier she wanted to become. The transition to civilian life was proving hard, and sometimes she couldn't be bothered even to try it.

'Then one morning, out of complete frustration I realised I needed to stop feeling sorry for myself and get back in the gym. The doctors said I could start training again, but slowly.' She ditched the pizzas and began eating healthily again. Food, health, training: these were things she could control. She stopped thinking of all the things she couldn't do with her injury and instead thought of all the things she could do.

Though she was no longer in the forces, her background there wasn't entirely wasted. At a networking event run by the Officers' Association she got talking to a man who offered her a job at the online food delivery company Deliveroo – 'Soon I was running live ops, monitoring squads of delivery drivers and riders all across London in real time. OK, it wasn't quite like a proper naval exercise, but it was the next best thing!'

Her best friend had competed in the 2014 Invictus Games and had raved about the time she'd had there, so when Help for Heroes asked Zoe whether she wanted to be considered for selection for Orlando, she nearly bit their hand off. 'I knew straight away that I'd want to compete. Of course, I was nervous about trying out, but this felt like the opportunity I'd been waiting for. Something to give me a focus and purpose again. It was also a chance to prove to everyone – and myself – that I wasn't going to be defined by my injuries.'

Before joining the Navy, Zoe had been a synchronised swimmer for a decade, and had ended up representing Great Britain. Synchronised swimming is easy to laugh at, and lots of people do – the fixed grins, the waterproof make-up, the weird sequinned costumes and even weirder routines. But for those who do it, it's a hell of a tough sport. It's like sprinting for three and a half minutes while periodically holding your breath, and you have to remember complex routines and stay in perfect time with everyone else. If your nose clip comes off, it's over. If you run out of breath and you come up, it's over. If you touch the bottom, it's a penalty, and that means it's probably over.

This was the kind of resilience and experience Zoe could draw on. She trialled for the swimming events – she'd also swum for the Navy against the Army and RAF in inter-service championships – and also for indoor rowing. 'I'd never rowed before and had no idea what to expect. But a month later, I got the news that I'd made it into both teams – it was an incredible feeling.'

Zoe began training with single-minded purpose – 'It was time to grit my teeth, put my head down and focus on what was ahead.' The swimming drills she was used to, but rowing was a different matter: as every oarsman and woman will tell you, sometimes you give so much that even your eyelashes hurt.

'The mental challenge to keep going when I was in pain was incredibly tough. One day, I was on the rowing machine feeling like my back was going to completely seize up and I saw videos of rowers in other countries who were due to compete being posted all over social media. That was my turning point. I thought: "If they can do it, so can I."'

From the moment she arrived in Orlando, she was swept up by the 'incredible atmosphere. It was amazing, it really was.' But she was also there to take her events seriously. Before her events she had her game face firmly on: total concentration, no waving to the crowd or goofing around. 'I get really bad nerves, I absolutely hate standing on the blocks, but as soon as I'm there, coiled back and ready to dive into the pool, I forget about everything else.'

She won three golds and a silver: 'Holding those medals for the first time will stay with me forever. The whole experience will. I've never seen a competition like the Invictus Games: everyone gets behind each other, no matter where you're from. I proved to myself that my injury didn't define me and that I could still achieve significant things regardless of the limitations I faced. That part of my life which injury had taken away from me – I'd got it back.'

5

THE FELL CLUTCH OF CIRCUMSTANCE

Three snapshots of a prince.

September 1997. Not quite yet a teenager, Harry walks behind his mother's coffin. His fists are balled by his side and he stares straight ahead. He walks with his brother, his father, his grandfather and his uncle. His brother William is already as tall as the adults, but Harry is a head shorter, a break in the line which draws your eye. More words have been written about this day and the ones which preceded it than about any other week in modern British history, and amid the whirling vortices of public emotion and devotion, of recrimination and accusation, nothing is purer and simpler and more important than the fact that these two boys have lost their mother, and your heart breaks for them over and over.

Fast forward 10 years: September 2007. The halo is somewhat tarnished: allegations of underage drinking and smoking dope, clashes with paparazzi, wearing a Nazi uniform with a swastika to a fancy dress party. The sanctimonious members of the public, of which there are millions, chunter away about spoiled rich kids, irresponsibility and Hooray Henrys. The more charitable members of the public, of which there are also millions, recognise that this is a young man growing up in an unrelenting and unforgiving media spotlight, and that few of us would come out smelling of roses if every one of our youthful indiscretions was splashed across the front pages.

Fast forward another 10 years: September 2017. On the eve of the Toronto Invictus Games, Harry's charm, charisma, decency, empathy and sense of fun win people over wherever he goes. You can see it in the way they respond to him: not the reverential and deferential forelock-tugging of old, but a genuine happiness to be in his presence, to hold their hands to his incandescent warmth, to be sprinkled with his stardust.

So what changed?

On one level, nothing, apart from the obvious: the passage of time and a young man maturing. He's always been loyal, generous, gregarious and a good friend to people. But between the second and third snapshots came the bulk of his service in the Army, including both his combat tours, and it's hard to dismiss this as pure coincidence. It wasn't just that the Army gave Harry what he'd always sought, the chance to prove himself, and that his fellow soldiers – who have a lower tolerance for bullshit than almost any other group of people – accepted him for the man he is rather than the title he bears.

It was also that he was genuinely good at his job. On his second tour of Afghanistan in 2012–13, he co-piloted Apache helicopters. Any idea that this was some kind of sinecure is ludicrous. Only the very best pilots in the Army Air Corps (AAC) get onto the Apache programme. And they're rated not just on their own skill but on their effect on their colleagues. Lt Col David Meyer, who oversaw Harry's training before that deployment, says, 'Harry's course – and I do genuinely believe it had a lot to do with his influence – was incredibly well-galvanised and they tended to galvanise around him. That was one of his key strengths, as he wasn't better than anyone else at flying or anything like that, but he just understood the whole team ethic, how to win together.'

He just understood the whole team ethic, how to win together. Could there possibly be a better description of what the Invictus Games are all about?

In May 2013, the Prince attended the Warrior Games in Colorado Springs. The Warrior Games are an annual multi-sport event for wounded, injured and sick Service personnel, and this was their fourth edition. 'I was hooked,' Harry wrote in the *Sunday Times* in August 2014. 'It was one of the most incredible and inspiring things I had ever seen. It made me appreciate the simple things in life, the things we take for granted. Some of those competing had been lying in a bed no more than eight months earlier, being told they would never walk again, and now here they were, winning medals in front of a community of supporters. The passion, determination, teamwork, resilience, inspiration and just downright fun oozed out of this competition.'

There were two problems. First, the competitors were almost exclusively American, with only a handful of British invited. Second, competitors pretty much outnumbered spectators. There were only a few hundred watching from the stands, and no wider coverage worth the name – no TV cameras, precious little social media. And all this in the country which reveres its military more sincerely and openly than anywhere else in the Western world.

The execution of the Warrior Games might have left something to be desired, but there was nothing wrong with the central concept. It was a good idea, it was a *great* idea. And Harry knew there was only one thing to do with an idea as good as this.

Steal it.

Actually, the Warrior Games were an older idea than they seemed. The North-West of England Limbless Sports Club had held a sports day for disabled ex-servicemen as far back as 1922. It had been opened by Earl Haig, who had commanded British forces on the Western Front during the Great War, and included football, obstacle courses, high jump and 'a well-contested walking race'. Interestingly, the day's two main remits seem to have been the promotion of sport as part of recovery programmes and the showcasing of the latest technology in prosthetic limbs.

Sport as rehabilitation for injured servicemen was also the focus during World War Two of the neurosurgeon Ludwig Guttmann, who established a spinal injuries treatment centre at Stoke Mandeville hospital. Dr Guttmann organised the Stoke Mandeville Games, which began in 1948, and in 1960 they were for the first time held alongside that year's Olympic Games in Rome and became the Paralympics. (The mascot for the London 2012 Paralympics was called Mandeville.)

'If ever I did one good thing in my medical career,' Guttmann said on retirement, 'it was to introduce sport into the treatment and rehabilitation programme of spinal cord sufferers and other severely disabled.'

But what Harry had in mind was much larger than either of those events had been, at least in their early incarnations. Just because it had been done before didn't mean it would be easy to do again.

Before firing a weapon, Apache pilots ask themselves three questions: Can I? Should I? Must I? Only when the answer to all three is yes, do they fire. When it came to the Invictus Games, it was these same three questions which needed to be asked and answered (under slightly less time and situational pressure than an Apache pilot usually gets, granted).

Can I?

If anywhere could host an international sporting event at short notice, it was London. The year before the 2013 Warrior Games, the city had hosted what was by common consent the greatest Olympic and Paralympic Games of modern times. Even the Australian press, who were justifiably proud of the show that Sydney had put on in 2000 and hand out praise to the Poms through gritted teeth, conceded as much. 'As awful as it is to admit,' said *The Australian*, 'London 2012 was bigger, slicker, almost as friendly and more thoughtfully planned than Sydney ... There is one simple indication of the success of the past two weeks. That is the feeling of surprise among ordinary Londoners and people close to the Games that after all that anticipation and all their doubts, they had pulled it off so well. It is not a sense of "We told you so", more one of "My God, we actually did it!"'

Everywhere you looked during those two weeks, you saw magic. The main stadium was packed full, day and night:

90,000 people were there even for the morning sessions, which were just heats rather than finals. There was the Dorney Roar out at the rowing lake: the pressure waves of 30,000 screaming voices reverberating across the water in a sport where some regattas attract one man and his dog and you're lucky if the dog turns up. The stillness and beauty of the archery at Lord's cricket ground, as iconic a sporting arena as the country has to offer. And of course that glorious, madcap, bonkers, exuberant Opening Ceremony, whose most iconic moment had been a certain grandmother leaping from a helicopter with a reasonably famous secret agent.

One of the reasons behind the Games' success had been the Army itself. All the military talk beforehand had been of terrorist threats and missiles being stationed on the roofs of tower blocks. Then, with literally a couple of days to go, the contractor G4S had admitted it couldn't provide all the security personnel it had been contracted to provide. Into the breach had stepped the Army, and in doing so had snatched victory from the jaws of disaster.

The soldiers were exactly what was needed: bright and breezy, cheery and friendly, their kaleidoscope of accents proudly heralding that this may have been London but it was a tournament for the whole country. They checked bags and manned metal detectors with slick thoroughness, and yet you knew that if by that million-to-one chance the worst did happen, there was no one else in the world you'd want dealing with it. The spectators loved them.

But it had not necessarily always been that way. It would have been interesting, for example, to have seen the public's reaction to uniformed soldiers at Olympic venues had Manchester won either of its 1996 or 2000 bids to host the Games. But in the few years before the Olympics, public sentiment had swung firmly behind the actual soldiers in combat, even – especially – when attitudes towards the conflicts themselves were ambivalent. You might have opposed the political rationale for intervention in Afghanistan or Iraq, but you still recognised the bravery and profession-alism of the boys on the ground doing the job.

The first real sign of this sea change came in the summer of 2007, when members of the Royal British Legion in the town of Wootton Bassett began to formally pay their respects to the Union Jack-covered coffins of British soldiers passing through the town en route from RAF Lyneham to the John Radcliffe Hospital in Oxford. The simple dignity of the gesture struck a chord, and soon hundreds or even thousands of ordinary citizens were lining the route, which in turn made national headlines on the evening news.

Not that television was merely reflecting the change: it was driving it too. If the embedding of journalists with front-line troops had been a first step in showing something of the reality of war, then the extraordinary series of documentaries which the actor Ross Kemp filmed in Afghanistan from 2008 onwards took this forward several steps. Watching Kemp and his crew filming a real-life contact between Royal Anglian soldiers and the Taliban – filming it right on the spot, not from a mile away – yanked audiences from the comfort of their living rooms and made them feel that they were there with them. The crack of the bullets – they sounded like nothing ever heard in a movie, that was for sure – the urgency of the men scrambling for position and returning fire, the gut-clenching fear but also the supercharged excitement, it all came bursting out of the screen.

Kemp deliberately steered away from the usual conventions of traditional documentary. There was no discussion of Western policy in Afghanistan, no attempt to fix the narrative within a wider discourse and no concession to 'balance' by matching supporters of the war with its opponents. His focus was on the men in theatre, and on them alone: 'What we tried to show was what the ordinary soldiers are facing, what they are going through. I have seen incredible bravery from very young guys, the young generation that people write off. Look what they are doing in Helmand, and they are doing it for such appallingly low pay. Others in public services – nurses, teachers, the police – have a voice. These guys don't and I hope I can help. We tried to show the reality they are facing on the ground. They're not asking for sympathy, just a little respect, and they certainly deserve that.'

His rapport with them was genuine, as was the banter: the soldiers took the mickey mercilessly for his role as SAS Sergeant Henno Garvie in the ITV series *Ultimate Force*, and he gave it back with interest. But as much as the whizz-bang spark of contact it was the quiet moments which stayed with you, none more so than seeing how the men seemed to age years in just months of deployment: thinner, more weathered, more prone to the thousand-yard stare. The news could give the impression that 21st-century war was fought almost exclusively by remote, video game-style. Kemp's footage showed that not only was this not true, but that stifling heat and the constant threat of landmines, IEDs, enemy snipers, rocket-propelled grenade (RPG) attacks and even friendly fire took a severe and very real toll.

A gentler counterpoint came in the winter of 2011, when the nation's favourite choirmaster, Gareth Malone, went to the Royal Marine Barracks at Chivenor in Barnstaple, Devon – not for the Marines themselves, but for their wives. Anyone who'd seen the preview tapes would have been well advised to buy shares in Kleenex! Malone took a bunch of women who hardly knew each other and who in many cases felt defined by who their husbands were. He transformed them into not just a sisterhood but a choir of genuine talent and emotion. When he auditioned for soloists, he was look-ing for those whom the whole group supported rather than setting singer against singer. It was collaboration rather than competition, and a rare insight into what wives and girl-friends go through while their men are away for months at a time. Their single 'Wherever You Are' ended up as the Christmas number one that year, with proceeds from the sales going to the Royal British Legion and SSAFA Forces Help.

So yes, Harry could stage the kind of Games he had in mind: both the public support and the infrastructure were there.

Should I?

There would certainly be no shortage of people eligible to compete. One of the knock-on effects of the extraordinary advances in battlefield medicine was that many more people were surviving than had ever been the case before. This is not comparing Afghanistan with the Falklands or Vietnam or World War Two: this is comparing Afghanistan 2009 with Iraq 2003, for example, because that's how fast the game was being moved on.

Harry knew that this progress came at a price. In that *Sunday Times* article of August 2014, he wrote: 'With survival ... come higher rates of life-changing injuries – whether visible or invisible. They are injuries that the news will forget, injuries that we will all forget as the world moves on to the next conflict or natural disaster. But those limbs will not grow back, friends will not return and many will be left with horrifying images and memories ingrained on their minds. It is hard for any of us to comprehend what these guys have been through.

'There is no comparison to the scale of other conflicts, the Great War, for example, and I understand that – but one life is just as important as 10. They were someone's father, brother, son, daughter, sister, mother. I have often thought: how do you get over that? How do you move on and clear your mind of such painful images? How does someone who has lost a limb find the motivation to move on and avoid being defined by that injury: to be recognised for their achievements, not just given sympathy post-injury?'

This was the crux. There was no point doing it unless the competitors would benefit, and Harry was in no doubt that they would: 'I saw [at the Warrior Games] the power that sport could play in the recovery of both mind and body. Sport is surely the best way to support recovery. The premise is simple: set yourself a target, take your mind off all the negative thoughts and concentrate on the challenge in front of you, all while relearning to use your body.'

The Invictus Games would be a way of aiding recovery rather than an end in itself. If some of the competitors also became Paralympians then that would be great, but that would never be the intention. Participation would always be more important than sheer performance (in fact, the increasingly elite performances in the Paralympics were leaving more room for an Invictus-style Games). Someone battling the daily fires of post-traumatic stress or the difficulties of life as a triple amputee would not suddenly find themselves cured by competing at the Invictus Games. But the experience *would* help them on their path back to as normal a life as possible, and this would hold true no matter whether they were two days or two years into a rehab course.

It wasn't just the physical aspect of the Games which appealed to Harry, but the mental and social ones too. There is always a void when one retires from active service, and that void yawns deeper and wider when retirement has been forced on you in your prime. The Invictus Games would fill that void. It would offer, if only for a few days, the things which its competitors had been missing: their country's flag on their chest or left arm, being part of a team, the quickfire dark humour, the camaraderie. It would give them that military fix which they yearned for; it would not patronise nor infantilise them. If they needed help, it was the help to let them help themselves. Allowing them that was as crucial as any minutely measured conventional progress towards rehabilitation.

But the rehab aspect was not all that mattered, or else they could have held the Games in a sports centre on an RAF base. The whole point of taking it out to the public was to allow the people to show their support for, to paraphrase George Orwell, the men and women who let us sleep soundly in our beds because they stand ready in the night to visit violence on those who would do us harm.

It would be a chance for the public to say thank you and for the competitors to put on a show for them: a perfect feedback loop of spectator and gladiator. And therefore it wouldn't be just the competitors who reaped the benefit. Someone sitting in the stands seeing the inspirational stories being played out right in front of them: who knew what effect that might have? Or someone watching on television at home, maybe someone disabled, who would see these men and women and think they could follow suit. Who knew whose lives might be changed by what they saw rather than what they did?

So, yes, Harry should hold the Games, of course he should.

Must I?

In some ways this was the easiest one to answer of the three. If he could, and he should, then surely he must? Indeed: but in this case the emphasis was as much on the 'he' as the 'must'. It is not fanciful to suggest that the Invictus Games would simply not have happened without Harry. No one else, literally no one else, had what he had: the royal title, the military experience and the natural charm. There were those who had two of the three, but only he had the lot. He knew he was in a fortunate position, one which came with a name and a lineage and access to all sorts of different areas. He also knew that he had a responsibility to use that position in a positive way, in the right way.

The Invictus Games would be different because it would be forged not perhaps strictly in his own image but certainly according to his own values. It would be fiercely competitive, but it would also be fun. It would leave no man or woman behind: there would be medals of gold, silver and bronze, but there would also be medallions for every competitor in recognition that for many it was the start line rather than the finish line which was the real achievement.

Most of all – and the comparisons with his mother are very clear here – it would be Harry giving a voice to the damaged and the forgotten, just as he has in Lesotho by setting up the Sentebale charity with Prince Seeiso of Lesotho to benefit orphans and vulnerable children, many of whom are affected by the country's HIV/AIDS epidemic. Harry is very good at making connections with people and putting them at their ease. Part of this is the fact that he's tactile and relaxed, a normal person in an abnormal position. But it's also because he's genuinely interested in people: he wants to know their stories, he wants to know what makes them tick. He looks out for them. His emotional intelligence is extraordinary.

I saw a small example of this when I went to talk with him for this book. It was an unseasonably warm day in March, and early on in our chat I quickly wiped my forehead with the back of my hand. Harry was answering a question at the time, but without breaking his reply he got up, went over to the window, opened it, came back and sat down. It was a minor thing, sure, but what was interesting was what he didn't do as much as what he did. He didn't draw attention to my (very mild) discomfort by asking me if I was OK. He didn't ask anyone else in the room to open the window. He just got up and did it: thoughtful, scrupulously polite and totally without airs and graces.

Can, should, must … The Games were on.

Now all Harry had to do was organise them. And he knew the best man for the job: Sir Keith Mills, the man who had invented Air Miles and had more latterly been deputy chairman of LOCOG, the London Organising Committee of the Olympic Games and Paralympic Games.

They met in November 2013. Harry said he wanted the Games to be held the following year, 2014, and in the interests of the competitors it shouldn't be too deep into winter. September seemed like a good month. How about September?

September was possible, Mills said. But with no venues and no funding yet in place – at that stage there was literally nothing other than two men talking in a Kensington Palace drawing-room – it'd be tight. It would be *very* tight. They were looking at an event only 10 months away. Harry would have to be involved every step of the way. 'If we're going to do this,' said Mills, 'you really need to be hands-on and involved. You can make things happen more quickly than I can.' But Harry didn't even need asking. He wanted to be in among it just as he had been in the Army, feeling the team working together. In fact, he quit active duty military service in January 2014 to devote himself to the Invictus Games full-time.

Neither the competitors nor the spectators would have given this much thought, and understandably so, but events like the Invictus Games don't happen just like that. They take an extraordinary amount of organisation across a multitude of different areas.

Corporate sponsorship was the obvious avenue for the bulk of the money needed, but at such short notice that was easier said than done. Most corporations had their budgets for the next 12–18 months already sorted and signed off, and even the largest and wealthiest companies can't just find the odd million or three stuffed down the back of the sofa. In came Jaguar Land Rover as official presenting partner and

BT, Fisher House Foundation, Ottobock, PwC and YESSS Electrical as Official Supporters. The Royal Foundation of The Duke and Duchess of Cambridge and Prince Harry and the Ministry of Defence were the founding partners of the 2014 Invictus Games.

Next, they needed a name. Numerous suggestions were bandied around, many of them variations on recognisably military words – 'soldier', 'warrior', 'army' and so on – until Major-General Buster Howes, the Defence Attaché at the British Embassy in Washington, DC, who had first invited Prince Harry to the Warrior Games, suggested 'Invictus'.

Invictus had most recently been a Clint Eastwood film about post-apartheid South Africa's famous victory in the 1995 Rugby World Cup, starring Morgan Freeman as Nelson Mandela (a role he had surely spent much of his life waiting for) and Matt Damon as a surprisingly convincing Francois Pienaar. The title – the word *invictus* is Latin for 'unconquered' – had come from a poem of the same name by the Victorian writer William Ernest Henley, which Mandela liked to read both to himself and his fellow prisoners during his decades of confinement on Robben Island.

UNCONQUERABLE

Out of the night which covers me,
Black as the pit from pole to pole,
I thank whatever gods may be
For my unconquerable soul.

In the fell clutch of circumstance
I have not winced nor cried aloud.
Under the bludgeoning of chance
My head is bloody, but unbowed.

Beyond this place of wrath and tears
Looms but the horror of the shade,
And yet the menace of the years
Finds, and shall find me, unafraid.

It matters not how strait the gate,
How charged with punishments the scroll,
I am the master of my fate:
I am the captain of my soul.

As a summary both of what the competitors had been through and the values they still held dear, it was note perfect. And so 'Invictus' it was: the Invictus Games.

As for the 'brand' itself, getting that right was absolutely crucial. Harry wanted it not just to capture the spirit of the event but also to be cool and funky, something you'd actively aspire to wear rather than just shrug it on without being especially bothered one way or the other. The logo that was created, picking out 'I AM', so prominent in the last two lines of Henley's poem, from the middle 'I' of 'Invictus' and the 'AM' of 'Games', was spot on.

But the success or failure of the Games would ultimately rest on a group of people who'd been scarcely involved with all this frantic preparation. Indeed, some of them hadn't even heard about the Games until a few months beforehand.

They were, of course, the competitors.

FABIO TOMASULO, ITALY

Fabio Tomasulo was mad keen on flying as a child. He was determined to join the Italian Air Force, even if he had to go in as a computer programmer or a mechanic rather than as a pilot. Aged 20, he became the first person in his family to join the military when he signed up for the Air Force, just as he had always dreamed of.

Over the next decade and a half he held many different positions, including Section Head at the office of the Deputy Chief of Air Staff. Then early in 2007 he was in a car accident so severe that he needed to have his left leg amputated just below the knee: 'The first few days in the hospital were very traumatic, especially psychologically. Suddenly I missed all those certainties that had brought me up to that point in my life. Will I be able to walk again? Can I resume my work? Can I support my family? These were the thoughts that plagued me day and night.

'Then slowly, day after day, thanks above all to the support of my family, I started slowly to glimpse the light at the end of the tunnel. After two operations I started to walk with a prosthetic leg. More than a year after the accident, I was able to return to work with the same rank as before.'

Before the accident Fabio had been a keen sportsman: 'I liked running and spinning, just to keep fit.' But when Invictus came knocking in 2014, he decided not to do a sport he knew well but one which was totally new to him: 'Archery had always fascinated me, but until then I'd never had the opportunity to try it. It was love at first shot! Right from the moment the first arrows left the bow I knew I loved this sport. I don't know if I chose archery or if archery chose me.'

Three months of intensive training later, he came home from London with a gold medal in the individual novice category: 'I will never forget the amazing emotion of receiving the gold medal. Going up to the top step of the podium, wearing the colours of my nation – just thinking about it brings tears to my eyes.' Two years later in Orlando, by now too experienced to still be classed a novice, he won a bronze in the individual open competition and another bronze medal in the team event.

Fabio is still an active officer. He has the rank of Lieutenant Colonel and is now Section Head Individual and Aquatic Sports at the Air Force Sports Centre – 'As they say, the appetite comes with eating, and since I have the opportunity to train every day my passion for archery is still increasing. It makes me forget that I have a disability. Sport, particularly in a situation like ours, allows you to come out of your shell. Many of us hide behind what happened. Sport makes you feel alive.

'Participating in the Invictus Games was really exciting and amazing, not just from the purely sporting aspect, but especially from the human point of view. Being able to share experiences with other soldiers, men and women who have suffered traumas and disabilities like me, was really significant and important, and it helped me to accept what had happened to me and to definitively overcome it.

'Besides the spirit of sport, there is a brotherhood among us because we are all soldiers who have suffered injuries. And it is a way to share what we have become after injury. I remember as if it were yesterday all the people who cheered during the competitions and thanked us for what we had suffered for serving our country. It is an indescribable emotion that I will carry in my heart for the rest of my life. We are not what life has given us, but we are what we will do in our lives.'

6

NOT WINCED NOR
CRIED ALOUD

Even at nine o'clock in the morning, the Sports Training Village at the University of Bath is a hive of activity. This is a £30m complex, and it shows. There's an Olympic-size swimming pool, a vast multi-sports hall which can be partitioned by thick curtains, a gym boasting every conceivable variety of weights and machines, an eight-court indoor tennis complex, a judo dojo, treatment rooms, hypoxic chambers that simulate conditions at altitude, and so on. And that's just what's inside.

The walls are dotted with posters outlining 11 qualities of successful athletes: aggressiveness, coachability, conscientiousness, determination, emotional control, drive, leadership, mental toughness, responsibility, self-confidence and trust. It's part internet inspiration quotes, part haiku and part socialist exhortation. Tracksuited men and women sit in the café with their protein shakes and recovery meals while analysing their sessions on laptops: heart and soul reduced to the pitiless basics of data. It's a long way from the days when rehydration in university sports was the preserve of Messrs John Smith and Gerard Heineken, and when a fitness freak was someone who lit up a Silk Cut before and after a match, but not at half-time as well.

These state-of-the-art facilities are not just for the university. The British national skeleton, bobsleigh and pentathlon teams have permanent bases here, and plenty of rugby, soccer and Olympic teams have used the place for training. Today there's a county tennis tournament, Southampton FC's youth academy players are here too – oh, and a training camp for those hoping to be in the British Invictus Games team for Toronto 2017.

The Invictus Games triallists aren't hard to spot. They're older than most of the other people here, and they have more tattoos and fewer limbs. But no one gives them a second glance. If you're here then you're here to work, and it doesn't matter who you are. A high-performance elite sports centre is surprisingly egalitarian in many ways.

On the way out to the athletics track, I pass a poster with a Muhammad Ali quote: 'Champions aren't made in gyms. Champions are made from something they have deep inside them – a desire, a dream, a vision. It's the lack of faith that makes people afraid of meeting challenges, and I believed in myself.'

It's cold outside and the track is still in winter order: the steeplechase water jump empty and covered over, the barrier removed. Far from the bright lights of summer night competitions, this is where the real work is done. There are two groups of people on the infield. Half a dozen women, including Mary Wilson, are inside the discus cage, participants in an impromptu ballet of demonstrating techniques and giving each other tips.

Outside the cage, a similar number of men wait their turn. A wheelchair is parked up against a sturdy steel frame for throwers who have lost their legs: the frame is lashed to the ground and the thrower is strapped to the frame. The men chat and blow on their hands. They keep up a constant stream of good-natured abuse to the women, and get it back in spades. No standing on ceremony for the fairer sex here. If you're here it's because you were in the Forces, and if you were in the Forces then you take the mick and you give it too. Soldiers are very equal opportunity like this; they take the piss out of everybody.

One of the women mistimes her throw. It slaps into the inside of the netting and drops to the ground. 'I'll give you a tip,' says one of the men. He has two artificial legs. 'You've got to get it out of the net.'

'And I'll give you a tip,' she replies. 'Never eat yellow snow.'

They all laugh. The women keep practising while the men rub their arms for warmth. Eventually the same man as before says in mock-exasperation: 'Right, that's it. Time's up, I'm putting my foot down.'

She's quick as a flash: 'Last time you did that it went "boom".'

They all laugh again, louder and more raucous. The notion of sport as a substitute for war is one of the oldest clichés in the book, but it doesn't seem too fanciful right now. You can see it in the way these men and women move around each other, instinctively aware of how much space they need, of where they can aim a good-natured arm punch and where they can't. They're back with their own kind, people who know and understand but don't stare or judge.

On the track, three men with prosthetic sprint blades jog gently round the bottom bend. They've left their everyday prosthetics leaning neatly against a wall – they change legs as easily as you or I change shoes and socks – and they carry themselves high on the 'balls' of their blades, which flex on every stride with the impact of landing and release.

As they jog, a handful of the Southampton FC Academy kids watch them go. These boys aren't yet teenagers, and right now their heads must be full of dreams of professional football and all that comes with it: the crowds, the fame, the nights of triumph and defeat, the money, the nightclubs, the cars, the girls. Yet most of them won't make it. Some of them will almost certainly end up in the Army (or perhaps the Navy, being Southampton), and they'll be deployed to whichever war we're fighting by then, where they may lose their legs just like these men have. I wonder if any of those boys are looking at their future without realising it.

The previous day, Leicester City had sacked Claudio Ranieri, the manager who only nine months before had led them to that unbelievable and unforgettable Premier League title. Watching the Southampton lads watching the Invictus Games amputees, it was hard not to imagine the whole thing as a morality tale for our times – a nice, decent man dismissed by people for whom results and profit are the most important things, while here blokes who had taken a year or two to earn what even a lowly Premier League journeyman makes in a week are running round a track for their own reconstruction rather than for money. Perhaps Ranieri would have enjoyed the company here more than at Leicester's King Power Stadium.

I go back inside: past another poster, this time quoting Sebastian Coe: 'There is a truth to sport, a purity, a drama, an intensity, a spirit that makes it irresistible to take part in and irresistible to watch.'

The swimming pool echoes with the coaches' instructions and the splashing of the water. On the far wall, kayaks are racked upright in line like sentries. There are two dozen Invictus Games swimmers here, many of them in Help for Heroes swimming caps. They do drills at their own pace, and that pace varies widely. Zoe Williams is among the first to do every length, scything through the water with a dolphin's grace. Mike Goody follows her. 'When I'm in the water I feel free,' he says, 'free with my thoughts. Alone with the water rushing over my ears, it's a unique sound. For me, that's just heaven.'

The pool does a pretty good job of hiding impairments: a one-legged swimmer is a lot less obvious than a one-legged runner. But this only goes so far. Bringing up the rear of the armada is a triple amputee. It's so hard to envisage swimming with just one arm and no legs that it takes me a moment or two to compute that he's doing just that. He lurches half out of the water with each stroke, a technique designed to keep him going in a straight line rather than crabbing off to one side. The strength, the skill, the mental fortitude to do this – not just one length, but the entire training session, swim and rest, swim and rest, swim and rest, no exceptions – is extraordinary, even by Invictus Games standards.

It seems fitting that the next poster I see is one quoting Arthur Ashe: 'You are never really playing an opponent. You are playing yourself, your own highest standards, and when you reach your limits, that is real joy.'

You can hear them before you see them – the hum and hiss of two dozen ergometer rowing machines, lined up facing each other in one section of the sports hall. Ergometers are brutal, offering all the pain of actual rowing with none of its pleasure. A screen pitilessly charts all the important numbers as the competitor pulls: split time per 500 metres, stroke rate, distance travelled, time elapsed. The machine never lies, and the machine always wins.

Hannah Lawton, a coach with the GB Paralympic programme, prowls between the machines, chivvying the rowers on: 'Breathe! Keep going! Doing really well! Last 10!' When the session's finished, the rowers slump forward over their handles or reach with shaking hands for their water bottles. 'Blimey,' one splutters. 'I only came for a weekend away!'

'OK,' Hannah shouts. 'Ten minutes' break and we go again. Don't be late back.' She eyes a man at the far end of the row and smiles. 'Especially you, Lamin.'

Lamin laughs; he laughs a lot. He joined the Irish Guards from his native Gambia, and lost both legs and an arm in an IED blast in Afghanistan. When you're a triple amputee rowing isn't much easier than swimming as one. Rowing is a legs sport – the powerful quadriceps muscles usually provide about 60 per cent of a stroke's power – and, on the rowing machine at least, a symmetrical one. Doing it the way Lamin does – fixed seat and one-handed, his body and back twisting with every stroke – is very difficult. Yet he hammers away with rhythm and determination until the session's over and he can laugh again. His very presence in the room lifts people: a smile here, a joke there. It's no wonder the producers of BBC1's *DIY SOS* featured him and his family (he and his wife have five children) moving into a specially adapted house in Manchester in 2015.

While the competitors are taking their break, Hannah and her fellow coaches rearrange the ergos into different configurations. 'We get all kinds of different impairments here,' she explains. 'For Invictus Games purposes they're assigned to one of three categories. There's LTA, legs, trunk and arms: a full range of motion, more or less. Then there's TA, trunk and arms, for those who can't move their legs, whether they're paralysed or have prosthetics. And then there's A, arms only. Competitors in TA and A usually need to be strapped onto their seats.'

Break over, Lamin gets back on the ergo. He's in a group of four, with each ergo set at 90 degrees to the next so they form a cross. Hannah sets them a simple programme: go 'round the clockface' doing 500 metres as fast as they can, one at a time. The three who aren't sprinting have to keep rowing gently while encouraging the one on test. The moment one person finishes, the one to his left takes it up.

David Shardles, who was left paraplegic after a motorbike accident, gives his 500 the full beans: arms straining, eyes screwed shut against the pain. The others roar him on. When he finishes, Lamin raises his single hand – 'Good work, Dave. I'd clap you if I had a second hand.' Still getting his breath back, Dave grins and makes a fist. 'I'll give you a fuckin' second hand, sunshine.'

'I left the Army after my accident,' says Dave. 'Didn't want anything to do with it for years. But then I went to the first Invictus Games and saw what I was missing out on.' He won a bronze in the hand cycling in Orlando, and is now hoping to be selected for Toronto. 'I love coming to things like this …' He indicates Lamin. 'And seeing idiots like this one.'

Hannah makes them all finish with 10 minutes' alternate sprinting and paddling: one minute hard, one minute easy, repeated five times. 'Anyone got any questions?' she asks.

A hand goes up. 'Yeah, I do. Where do babies come from?'

As the rowers go through their last piece, Hannah indicates a couple of them. 'You have to look beyond the numbers. That guy over there, he's giving it the chat, but I can tell he's finding it hard. And that woman there – well, her stats aren't great to say the least, but she's better than she was a month ago. She'll be better still in a month's time, and most of all, going to Toronto would be really, really good for her.'

This is one of the things which separates the Invictus Games from other events. Hannah is used to working on the Paralympic programme, where athletes' achievements and capabilities are easier to quantify. Of course there's still a subjective element, or else she could just put everyone on the ergos and take the top scorers – temperament, teamwork and personality play their parts – but fundamentally at the Paralympics you take the best personnel you have.

The Invictus Games are different. It's more about participation than performance, and everyone in this room I talk to wants it to stay that way. Most countries adopt variations of the same mindset when it comes to selection. They ask what the Games can do for the competitor quite as much as what the competitor can do for the Games.

For example, the official Australian regulations require 'particular regard to an applicant's demonstrated ability for teamwork, work ethic and team cohesion ... [the team management] may use discretionary selection powers if they feel an applicant that may not be competitive will benefit physically or psychologically (or both) from exposure to the team environment and the Invictus Games competition'. Several people from various countries who went to London and/or Orlando have deliberately withdrawn themselves from consideration for Toronto so that someone else can have their place and hopefully experience the same benefits they did.

There's no guarantee that all the people at this training weekend will be selected for the British team: indeed, most of them probably won't. There are only 90 places in the team across all the events, but 770 people have put themselves forward for selection. So the selectors will inevitably end up disappointing far more people than they will please. Their hope is that disappointment will be tempered by the fact that the Invictus Games were always intended to be a milestone on the road to recovery rather than an end in itself.

All the people who've come to Bath are by definition on that road already. Their stories vary in details more than in essence. In the immediate aftermath of whatever wounding, injury or illness changed their life, they were at the point which Dante famously identified in the very first line of the *Divine Comedy*: 'midway through my life I found myself in a dark wood'. They found it easy to wallow and hard to motivate themselves. The less they did, the less confidence they had. Pulling themselves out of that stage was like pulling a foot out of deep mud.

The first trip to the gym was the most important: they lifted a few weights, they got a sweat on, they felt the joy and pain of working their body again. Then they began to progress, and with that came the discipline: stick with a programme, set goals, achieve those goals, set new ones. All these things exist for the competitors, whether or not they go to the Invictus Games, and all these things feed through into other aspects of the competitors' lives too. Yes, they're wounded, injured or sick, but they accept who they are and find a new normal.

This is what the competitors find now, and it's what they found before London and Orlando. That summer of 2014 before the first Invictus Games, Stephan Moreau trained like a professional: 'I was in France when I got the call saying I'd been selected for the Canadian team, and I didn't pick it up for days as I didn't have a roaming package. But when I found out, I was just so excited. I was doing two or three sessions at the University of Victoria. A friend owns a sports clinic and was treating me three or four times a week – physio, sports massage, that kind of thing – and all for free, because I was representing Canada.'

Even for those few months, Stephan lived the life of a full-time athlete, totally focussed on the upcoming Games. And the white heat of that focus, together with the way he could measure himself becoming physically stronger, made him feel better about himself all round.

The British contingent for those first Games were having similar experiences. Maurillia Simpson trained for three seated throws – shot-put, discus and javelin. 'To have something to turn to because I'd lost my dream of being a soldier and to be able to turn to sport as my main focus was really astonishing,' she said. It wasn't just that she had world-class training facilities right there on her doorstep, or that the Invictus Games were literally home turf for her, it was also thoughts of what had happened at the Olympic Park just two years before.

Places carry memories quite as much as people do, and at some frequency beyond the ken of human ears the Olympic Park still echoed with the roar of one-legged sprinter Jonnie Peacock tearing up the track en route to his 100m Paralympic title, and with the apotheosis of Super Saturday when within 45 minutes of each other a Somali immigrant, a mixed-race girl from Sheffield and a ginger lad from Milton Keynes had all won gold for a land of vibrant hope and multicultural glory.

Josh Boggi was cranking out the miles on his handcycle, fuelled by the memories of the Battlefield Bike Ride the year before and what that had meant to him: the triumph of finding he was better than he thought he was, the joy of being part of a team again.

Mike Goody was excited about the message the Games were giving out – 'The idea of the Invictus Games is to get people motivated. To be frank, if that message is going across it doesn't matter if I podium or not.' But he still wanted to be standing up there with a medal, make no mistake, and he was training like fury to give himself the best chance of ensuring that. To do otherwise would have been to sell not just himself short but the Games themselves, because it was the input which counted rather than the output. Everyone trained and only a few got medals, but no one got medals without training.

Mary Wilson had been one of the few British competitors at the 2013 Warrior Games, which had given Prince Harry the Invictus idea in the first place – 'I'd really enjoyed those Games. The Americans were competitive, but they had fun as well. I couldn't wait for Invictus, for drawing together all those nations.'

Stephan with his post-traumatic stress, Maurillia with her leg injury, Josh with his three amputated limbs, Mike with his missing leg and his post-traumatic stress, Mary with her MS – none of them were what they had once been. But they were what they were now: they were all adjusting to the new normal.

And for them, just as for all the men and women at Bath on the training weekend, that new normal is nearer the old normal than perhaps they first thought. Despite the severe nature of the impairments some of these men and women face, the principles behind their training are largely the same as for able-bodied athletes. The basic building blocks of general preparation target strength and endurance through methods such as overload, variation and specificity.

The pre-competition phase is high-intensity and technique-oriented, and gives way to 'peaking' for competition itself, with a tapering off in the days before to maximise rest and therefore performance. Of course there are many specific aspects which have to be tailored towards impaired athletes, but then again even the most elite able-bodied athletes have limitations: there is a ceiling to what the human body can achieve.

In the final analysis, it comes down to one simple principle: you train people by their ability, not their disability.

AMY BAYNES, NEW ZEALAND

Amy Baynes joined the New Zealand Navy by mistake. She was at an unemployment centre in her hometown of Invercargill and 'the recruiter just kind of talked me into it. He was very persuasive.' Within weeks, she was sent to Devonport for basic training – 'I was only 19, it was a complete culture shock.'

Over the following years she was deployed as a combat medic to the Arabian Gulf, Bougainville, Afghanistan and Banda Aceh, the closest major city to the epicentre of the earthquake which had caused the 2004 Boxing Day tsunami. Working out of a damaged field hospital with Australian Army medics as part of a joint ANZAC team, Amy treated Indonesian locals who'd been injured in the tsunami or during the aftershocks – 'It was pretty hellish. There were people who'd lost everything: their homes, their families, their livelihoods.'

It was also a reminder that as much of modern soldiering is civic reconstruction and aid work as it is combat missions. A few months before the tsunami, Amy had been in Afghanistan. On patrol one day, she'd slipped on a slope, fallen awkwardly and landed on her hip – 'It started to get more and more painful in Indonesia and afterwards, but I just ignored it.'

At least she ignored it until the agony was such that she could no longer do so. In 2007 she underwent hip surgery and then a total hip replacement in 2013. Amy was 33 – most people who have hip replacements are twice that age. She also needed surgery on her back after finding out that she'd torn four of her vertebrae, the lowest of which was pressing down on her spinal cord – 'It was miserable. I couldn't even bend down to pick up my kids.'

Shortly after her hip replacement, she was asked whether she wanted to be part of the New Zealand team at the 2014 Invictus Games. 'I had no real idea what the Games were all about or what they'd be like. None of us did. There were 14 of us on the first training camp, and only two women, but right from the start it felt like family.

'And then the Games themselves – my God! They were amazing.'

In London Amy was like in a kid in a candy shop. You name it, she did it – road cycling, indoor rowing, archery, wheelchair rugby, powerlifting. She won two bronze medals, in road cycling and powerlifting, but says, 'That was just the icing on the cake. It was the whole experience which was so great. It changed my mindset. I saw people worse off than me, much worse off, but they still got on the start line and smiled. It changed my life, it really did. People say that as a figure of speech, but I mean it literally.'

She became a motivational speaker, telling her story and that of Invictus to schools and women's groups – 'You could hear a pin drop.' And when Orlando came around and the New Zealand selectors asked if she'd go again, her reply was a big fat 'You bet!'

This time she won two silver medals in the cycling, one of them on her birthday. 'Prince Harry sang "Happy Birthday" to me and kissed me on the cheek. You couldn't have a better person pushing these Games. If anyone else had done it, it wouldn't have the same meaning. You see how his heart glows when he presents the medals.'

Amy also experienced the Invictus Games care for family members. She'd taken her husband, Ross, to London in 2014, who said: 'She's worked hard and she deserves it. I'm super-proud, I couldn't have a bigger smile on my face.' In Orlando she brought her sister, Rachel – 'She'd been there for me right from the moment I had my accident, when I didn't even know Ross. Without her support I wouldn't be here.'

Most of all, Amy was inspired by her children. The morning of her birthday in Orlando, when she'd won silver, she'd thought about pulling out of that day's race: 'I didn't think I had it in me, but I thought about my kids all the way round the course. I did it for them, they're my inspiration. They come and watch me training, and they think it's pretty cool when I come back with my medals. I'll hold onto that thought when they're grumpy teenagers and think that everything I do is wrong!'

Amy is still in the Navy: she has the rank of Chief Petty Officer and is a team leader and associate lecturer at the Defence Health School in Burnham. If she doesn't compete in Toronto, she still wants to go as part of the coaching and management staff: 'Of course I want to compete, but I also want someone else to have the chance to change their lives. The Invictus Games means everything. It's given me a purpose, it's given me focus. My mind and body feel good now. I feel I can still give to my country, which is why I joined the New Zealand Defence Force in the first place. Once you've got the Invictus spirit, you don't want to lose it.'

7

MY UNCONQUERABLE SOUL

On a mild night early in September 2014, Prince Harry officially opened the first Invictus Games. The previous months had been a whirlwind of organisation. The Organising Committee had worked with a furious passion to make it happen in a time frame many had thought impossible. Days had blurred into nights, weekdays had elided into weekends. They had known that they could not, must not, dare not fail. And now here they all were – competitors, spectators, organisers – in the Olympic Park.

Three military bands, each representing a different service – the Band of the Irish Guards, the Central Band of the RAF and the Band of Her Majesty's Royal Marines, Collingwood – played the national anthem together. The Red Arrows performed a typically spectacular fly-past. The Queen's Colour Squadron gave a rifle demonstration, the King's

Troop Royal Horse Artillery a display. The actor Idris Elba recited Henley's poem, with the final lines – 'I am the master of my fate, I am the captain of my soul' – reflected in the 'I AM' badges, which so many were wearing. The competitors paraded in by nation, with the home team coming in last to wild applause.

Michelle Obama sent a video message from Washington, DC. 'Some of the most inspiring moments I have had as First Lady are when I've met wounded warriors like so many of you,' she said. 'You tell me that you're not just going to recover but that you're going to thrive. You tell me you're not just going to walk but you're going to run marathons. So to all of the competitors here today I just want you to know how incredible you are. You're inspiring all of us, especially our young people. Inspiring them to believe that if we dig deeper, if we work harder and confront the adversity in our own lives with just a fraction of the courage you show every day, there is nothing we can't achieve. To all the family members and caregivers in the audience, I want you to know that your courage doesn't go unnoticed either. These heroes wouldn't be here today without you. And while I can't hide that I hope that Team USA won't bring home a few gold medals, I want you all to know how proud my husband and I are of you and how humbled we are by your example. So good luck, everybody, and have fun out there.'

Have fun out there. No one tells Olympians and Paralympians to have fun out there. It was just one of the ways in which the Invictus Games were different.

And now it was Harry's turn. He strode to the lectern wearing a dark blue suit and a Brigade tie. The crowd applauded. Some of the competitors gave him good-natured barracking. He smiled. It was that kind of evening, and it would be that kind of Games, exactly as he'd always wanted it to be. He cleared his throat.

'Over the past eight years, I have witnessed the whole cycle of life-changing injury. Evacuating soldiers and local Afghans to hospital, flying home from Afghanistan with some of those critically injured, meeting others in hospital coming to terms with life-changing injuries, and finally trying to keep up with 12 wounded veterans on our way to the South Pole. I can only begin to imagine how challenging the journey of recovery is, but the admiration I have for these men and women, to move beyond their injuries, is limitless.

'Last year I visited the Warrior Games in the United States. Seeing people who only months earlier had been told they'd never walk again now winning medals in front of their family and friends was breathtaking. I knew that anyone would be inspired by what these men and women had achieved – not just other servicemen and women, but all those adjusting to life post-injury. Each of them have come such a long way. Even making it to the start line is a huge achievement.

'Their stories are as amazing as they are unique. However, they all share one thing – sport. Sport has been the vehicle for their recovery, allowing them to channel their passion into what can be achieved rather than what can't. No longer are these inspirational men and women defined by their injury but as athletes, competitors and teammates.

'Over the next four days we will see some truly remarkable achievements. For some of those taking part this will be a stepping stone to elite sport, but for others it will mark the end of a chapter in their recovery and the beginning of a new one. Either way, you can be sure that everyone who takes to the track, pool or field of play will be giving it their all. I have no doubt that lives will be changed this weekend.

'It gives me great pleasure to welcome the 13 nations to London and to say how delighted I am that many of you are joined by your families, recognising the vital part they play in your recovery. The British public's support for our servicemen and women has been exceptional: I know they will show you the same over the coming days.

'Finally, I would like to thank you for the tremendous example you set. Your stories move, inspire and humble us. You prove that anything is possible if you have the will. Welcome to the Games. Welcome to Invictus.'

The Games proper began the next morning – Thursday 11 September, anniversary of an event which had led directly to the conflicts in Afghanistan and Iraq and therefore to the wounds and injuries which so many competitors there had suffered. The crowds for the athletics at Lee Valley were loud and appreciative, and Maurillia Simpson revelled in it. She won a gold and silver in the IF5 discus and shot-put (competitors are categorised according to the scope and severity of their injuries: Simi's leg was so bad that she couldn't stand unaided during the throws and therefore had to compete while strapped to a static frame).

Those few moments while she settled onto the frame, preparing her body and mind for one huge effort, with thousands watching her in an expectant hush, which exploded into a mighty roar when the implement flew from her hand and landed on the grass – those were moments she never thought she'd have: 'In all my wildest dreams I never expected to end up here. When I was 10 I shouted at the Queen that I was going to come and live where she does: now I'm stood up on the podium in front of her grandchildren. Surreal doesn't quite cover it.'

Mary Wilson won a bronze in the IF4 (wheelchair) discus, a sport she'd taught herself from scratch the year before. As UK team captain for the athletics squad, however, her focus had been more on her teammates than on herself, just as she'd had to be responsible for all her charges' mental health in Bosnia and Afghanistan: she was mother hen.

'Even though I'm out of the Forces, I still have the mentality that we'll always be there for each other. Even though most of us didn't know each other when we arrived, it was like a jigsaw fitting together. It's the unspoken rule: you look after each other, you're friends with each other and you just get on with it. For some of the team, self-belief was at a minimum. You have to know how to motivate them.'

There were the ones who were so jumpy that they needed calming down. Then there were those who were so overwhelmed by the whole occasion that they had withdrawn into themselves. Mary got them back to where they needed to be: in the right state of mind to go out there, do their best and, like the First Lady had said, have fun.

It wasn't just her own teammates she helped, either. Where the British and American teams were large and equipped with all kinds of kit, the Afghan team comprised half a dozen members of the Afghan National Army 'with almost nothing, no decent clothing'. Mary saw that one of them was shivering – September in London might have been mild to an Edinburgh girl, but not to an Afghan man – so she gave him her fleece: 'After that he would always smile at me.'

The crowd cheered for everyone. They cheered for Ricky Furgusson, who came last in the IT2 (above-knee amputee)

100m final after having trouble with one of his artificial legs. He had lost both legs, five fingers, his left eye and suffered severe facial disfigurement in an IED blast in Sangin, Afghanistan. 'I used to look like David Beckham back in his youth but unfortunately they took that away from me!' he said. 'I don't recall the five days before [the accident], let alone the day it happened. I'm not too fussed. Afghan's not the nicest place to remember anyway. It's been great to compete here. I was cheered to the line and cheered back, which was fantastic but I felt like a bit of an idiot – them cheering me even though I hadn't won!'

They cheered for Andy Grant when he won the IT1 (below-knee amputee) 1500m final. A die-hard Liverpool fan whose nickname in the Marines had been simply 'Scouse', he had had the Liverpool motto 'You'll Never Walk Alone' tattooed on his leg. When the surgeon amputated his leg, he'd given Andy some good news and some bad news.

Good news: the amputation had been a success.

Bad news: he'd had to cut through the middle of the tattoo, so it now read simply 'You'll Never Walk'.

For Andy, of course, that had merely been a challenge. Now he wasn't just walking again, he was winning gold in the metric mile, and in a time faster than most people with two legs could manage. Canada's James Macintyre finished last, almost a minute behind Andy, and the crowd cheered him just as loudly. Both men crossed the line with their arms aloft and their faces wreathed in smiles: that was the Invictus spirit for you.

The athletics took place all Thursday, and Friday saw the archery competition – the latter also featuring a special exhibition match for three archers whose injuries were so severe (they each had to use their mouths to draw back the bowstring) that they'd been unable to compete in the main competition. Daniel Crane of the USA beat his compatriot Tatiana Perkins and Briton Paul Vice by firing a 10 and a nine with two of his three arrows.

A 10 and a nine … with his mouth.

Like the athletics, the archery (both main and special competitions) had been great, full of sportsmanship and generosity amid the striving. But there was still a sense that the Games needed something truly spectacular, an event which would set the place aflame as a sporting spectacle in its own right.

On Friday evening they found it.

Much of what anyone needs to know about wheelchair rugby can be found in its one-word nickname: murderball. Players smash into each other with enough force to tip either their opponents or themselves clean out of their chairs and onto the floor. The wheelchairs themselves are specially made, sometimes of titanium, and are so bashed and dented that they look as if they've flown through an asteroid belt. Wheelchair rugby may be the only sport where a welder sits alongside the physio on the bench: one to repair the competitors, the other their machines.

It's emphatically not a game for the faint-hearted, and that's just the spectators. For the competitors, the brutality of the game is exactly what they love about it. Wheelchairs tend to bring out well-meaning infantilisation towards their users from the able-bodied – 'You all right there? Can I get you anything? Bless, you're so brave.' That kind of thing. Having some lunatic smash into you like a demented dodgem driver is the best antidote to this cotton-wool world.

It's called 'wheelchair rugby', but in fact the sport contains elements of several different other disciplines too. It's played on a standard basketball court (though with no baskets and slightly different markings), and like basketball, the players must either bounce the ball or pass it within a given period (they can pass it forwards, not just backwards as in normal rugby union). The ball itself is a regulation volleyball slightly over-inflated to provide a better bounce. Players score by crossing the goal line between two cones with the ball in their possession. Contact between wheelchairs is permitted – not half! – but contact between players is not. As in American football but not in rugby, teammates of the player in possession may block their opponents but may not hold them. Players are graded according to the extent of their disability and assigned a value from 0.5 (the lowest functional level) to 3.5 (the highest). Four players are on court at any one time and the total of their values cannot exceed eight. Women and men play together – the women are given no special treatment and certainly don't expect any.

The Invictus Games final pits the British against the Americans. More specifically, it pits two very different but equally talismanic captains against each other. The British captain Charlie Walker – 'Yes, it's rather an ironic name in the circumstances' – contracted meningitis in 2006 while training to be a bomb disposal technician. 'I nearly died and all that sort of business. But once I got better, my legs were still a mess. After about two years of operations trying to fix them, they amputated them both below the knee.'

Walker is stocky and bespectacled. His opposite number, Ryan McIntosh, has a close-cropped haircut and the muscle definition of the athlete and American footballer he was before stepping on a landmine in Afghanistan.

Walker is 34; McIntosh is a decade younger.

Walker is a tactical mastermind, always calculating; McIntosh is raw speed and brute physical intensity.

Walker is wily experience; McIntosh is impetuous youth.

Walker is ice; McIntosh is fire.

The Copper Box is packed, the crowd noise reverberating around the walls. It was 'the box that rocks' during the Olympics and Paralympics two years ago. It's rocking again now.

Game on.

First blood to the British with Geraint Price scoring within the first five seconds. McIntosh himself levels things up inside half a minute: 1–1. Extraordinarily, there will never be more than a goal in it from start to finish. Every time one team gets ahead, the other will claw it back.

Ben Steele is tipped out of his chair and put back in by an official. The US packs their defensive 'key' box near the goal line with the maximum three players allowed: the British go left, go back to the middle, go right. Walker is always at the heart of it, directing proceedings like a quarterback, searching for the way through with endless patience until he finds it. In the stands, Sir Clive Woodward and Jonny Wilkinson, two men who know a bit about able-bodied rugby, wince at some of the hits coming in. The intensity and the fitness aren't an awful lot less than they were used to in the white heat of a World Cup final.

At half-time it's 7–7. The crowd sing and chant as the coaches gather their players in huddles. Still anyone's game.

Early in the second half, and the US have two men in the sin bin (a minute off the court or until the next goal is scored, whichever is the sooner). Four players against two for the British, and they aren't going to pass up an opportunity like that. McIntosh, serving his bin for a foul, exhorts the crowd to give them some more noise. They don't need asking. McIntosh comes out of the bin and then immediately goes back in for another foul. He's playing right on the edge, and Walker, the wily old fox, is beckoning him to that edge and just a little bit beyond.

Prowling the sidelines, the coaches can hardly make themselves heard. There is a strange but unmistakable beauty to the way the players spin their chairs on a dime or ghost through gaps made by the blocking of their teammates.

Three minutes left. The British are 12–11 up. Stuart Robinson is in for a certain score which will put them two ahead for the first time – and as he crosses the line the ball spills from his grasp. He clutches at it, instinctively and despairingly, but it's gone. No goal. The US go up the other end, get a lucky break from a fumble in the British defence, and Jacob Rich glides over: 12–12.

Two minutes left. The crowd noise pulses eager and insistent, spectators feeding their energy to the gladiators in the middle and getting it back from them: an endless loop of crescendo and fade, crescendo and fade, sound and fury renewing themselves with every goal.

British possession. The US are still playing their key defence – a solid barrier of three men back in the box at their own end. They're not pressing the British in their own back-court or playing a high line, they're just letting them come and then setting them the puzzle: how do you get through the wall?

Walker has the ball – of course he does. Once more he twists and spins, back and forth, working the angles, watching the patterns, looking for the angle, the space. There it is, *there*, down the right-hand side. See the gap and take it. Walker gets to the line, but he's outside the cones. He flips the ball inside for Daniel Whittingham to score – but even as Whittingham turns to celebrate, the goal is disallowed (Walker was fractionally out of bounds before releasing the ball). The crowd groan. Still 12–12.

From one captain to another. McIntosh is off and flying down the right wing for the US. Price tracks him back, arm muscles burning as he strains to keep pace. Hector Varela is making tracks for the US on the inside. If McIntosh can get a clean pass then Varela will be in unopposed, and that might well be that. McIntosh goes for the pass. Price blocks, and gets a slap on the back from his skipper in appreciation.

One minute left. Next score will surely seal it.

Walker has it back on his own goal-line. McIntosh comes to challenge, hard and direct. Walker bounces him off and heads upfield, carving a long 'S' right and left to the halfway line. Ahead of him, his teammates are blocking their opponents like pirates repelling boarders. McIntosh is scrambling to get back in position.

Two men left for Walker to get past. Forty seconds on the clock.

He goes down the left. McIntosh, indefatigable, comes to challenge again. Walker fixes him on a collision course, and at the last moment swerves away just far enough to survive the contact. Now it's a straight race for the line with Varela, and Walker has the momentum. He crosses amid bedlam: 13–12. It was a solo try from one end to the other, but he could never have done it without his teammates' commitment to wheeling the blocking lines.

Thirty seconds left. Still just about time for the Americans to level it up and take the match to extra time. They go for a long Hail Mary pass. It bounces free and Walker – who else? – collects it and runs the clock down. The British are champions.

And the Invictus Games were officially alight.

They were alight for Josh Boggi, one of those who beforehand hadn't really known what to expect – 'I was a bit cynical at times. I always thought it would be fun, but I did wonder whether it would basically be a big sports day. Then we got to the Olympic Park for the opening ceremony and we were like, wow, this is a bit bigger than we thought.'

Soldiers are world-class blaggers, and Josh was no exception. He had talked his way into the ArcelorMittal Orbit Tower, which despite the best efforts of its owners is better known as the Helter Skelter, and found himself watching the opening ceremony while standing next to Seb Coe. Three days later, he won a bronze in the IHB1 handbike time trial and came fourth in the road race.

In between those two events came one of the Games' most enduring images. With a few hundred metres to go in the men's IRECB1 recumbent road race, three Britons – Rob Cromey-Hawke, JJ Chalmers and Paul Vice, the man who the previous day had fired an arrow with his teeth – were clear of the field. They were eyeing each other up, knowing that timing was key for the sprint. Go too soon and they'd burn themselves out while letting the others slipstream them and come past; go too late and the race would be over before they'd fully launched their attack. Three men playing cat-and-mouse with each other, trying to work out not just which one of them was freshest but work out the terrain too. Taking a tight line through a corner or hammering a slight uphill might make all the difference.

And then, as one, they decided not to race it out. It wasn't prearranged and it wasn't a stunt, it just seemed the right thing to do at the time. They linked arms and came across the line as one. Those with sufficiently long memories may have recalled Dick Beardsley and Inge Simonsen, joint winners of the first ever London Marathon in 1981, who had also decided on the spur of the moment to cross the line hand in hand after being unable to pull away from each other. Their gesture, like that of the three cyclists, had been an instinctive show of sportsmanship: respect not just for the opponent and the event, but the very spirit of togetherness which is at the heart of sport.

The Games were also alight for Mike Goody. Not because of the four gold medals he won, though of course he was proud of them, but because of what both swimming and the competition gave him. 'When I'm in that pool all my worries, all my negativity, just disappears. I'm at peace swimming side by side with my fellow comrades. The Games were great, everyone giving everyone shit the whole time. You make friendships all over the world, and of course you then connect on social media and keep those friendships going after you all return home.'

And they were alight, if that is not too inappropriate a word given what he had suffered, for Stephan Moreau. Competing in all three sprints in the IT6 (minor non-permanent injury) category, he'd failed to qualify from the heats of the 100m and 200m, but in the 400m final he was leading coming into the home straight only to have four other competitors run him down. But after a decade of illness and recovery – 'I didn't have hope, or I didn't think I had hope' – even being here was enough.

'It was unbelievable, the whole thing. From day one when we arrived at the airport, where we had our own special lane straight through the airport and police escorts right past all the traffic, we had people coming to us, introducing themselves to us and helping us. We were amazed by how well organised it was and how nice people were as well – it was a totally different level to what we expected. When I got together with the other athletes it was like we were friends straight away as you didn't have to explain your situation to each other. We understood each other well and it was really easy to be open with everyone here.'

Stephan also competed in the cycling, where he got one of the biggest cheers of the Games – 'It was the IRB3 road race. There was one British guy way off the front and he was gone for gold, but there were a few of us looking for silver and bronze. I was feeling good and in a group with a couple of guys from the Danish team, so we all decided to work together. Then I touched wheels with someone and went down.' He quickly got back on his bike – hence the crowd's cheer – but his chance of a medal was gone: 'The cleat on one of my shoes was broken so I took off that shoe and rode barefoot on that side.' Without the cleat to lock his foot into the pedal, Stephan couldn't apply as much power to the pedals, and found himself being overtaken. 'I was crushed, and I started crying – tears of frustration, yes, but also determination. Just keep going, I told myself. Just keep going.' Having been in the hunt for a medal, he ended up 17th, but there was some consolation at the end: the five Danish guys who had finished ahead of him enveloped him in a group hug.

That was the spirit of the Games right there: everyone looking out for each other and everyone equal, no matter who they were. Earlier on in the proceedings, Stephan had walked into one of the public toilets and been taken aback to see Prince Harry and Prince William in there. 'I couldn't believe it! I thought they'd be like rock stars, you know, with security clearing out the restrooms so they could use them in peace. But no, there they were, just – you know, normal. I really wanted to meet them, but I didn't think I could just introduce myself standing next to them at the urinals! So I thought "I'll hold it" and waited outside till they came out and I could introduce myself. And it was worth it. You can tell when high-profile people are there just to be there. Harry's not one of those – he's there because he really wants to be. It was serious and really mattered to him. It was personal, and to do it was a real mission for him. He's a great guy. I've got this picture with him and what I'll always remember was how he was just one of the guys.'

Mike Goody agreed. 'Harry was an absolute legend. He was everywhere. You know, we couldn't get rid of him if we tried. He was literally boosting everything, pumping everything, getting everyone going, really encouraging. He's proper sound.'

Wherever you looked over those four days in east London, there were remarkable people doing remarkable things, and perhaps none more so than Israel Del Toro. It wasn't his placing – 15th in the men's powerlifting with a lift of 80kg – which caught the eye. It was that DT – everyone calls him DT – could lift anything at all, having lost the fingers on both hands in an IED blast which also left him with burns to 80 per cent of his body.

His story is so extraordinary that Hollywood should make a movie of it, if only because no screenwriter would dare make up anything even remotely resembling the reality. DT lost both his parents before the age of 13: his father to a heart attack, his mother to a drunk driver. The eldest of four, he had to provide for his siblings while still trying to work out what he wanted to do with his life.

One day, he saw an Air Force advert on television, and shortly afterwards spoke with a 'very persuasive' recruiter. He was deployed to Iraq with the 82nd Airborne and awarded a Bronze Star for bravery in 2004's murderous Battle of Fallujah. A year later he went to Afghanistan, where, on 4 December 2005, his 'entire life changed'.

It was the third day of a patrol tracking Taliban fighters north of Kabul. 'We were crossing a creek in a Humvee [High Mobility Multipurpose Wheeled Vehicle] when we rolled over a pressure-plate IED. My body took the brunt of the blast and suddenly my entire world was fire. From head to toe, my body was engulfed in flames. I hit the ground and tried to pull myself out. All I could think about was that I was going to die here and never going to see my family again. Then the Lieutenant was grabbing me and dragging me back to the creek and extinguishing the flames.'

DT's own radio had melted in the fire, so he called over a private whose set was still working and ordered him to relay co-ordinates – not for the medevac to get him out and to hospital, but for airstrikes to complete the mission. Only once that was done did he call for the medevac. His last coherent thought before slipping into a four-month coma was a simple one: 'I wasn't going to let my three-year-old son [Israel III, known as 'Little DT'] know the pain of losing a father like I had.'

A four-month coma was bad enough; waking up from it even worse. When DT first passed a mirror and didn't recognise himself, he became terrified that his son wouldn't want to see him – 'That was the first and only time that I wished I had died. My wife, Carmen, and therapists convinced me that all he wanted was a father, and they were right.'

He was so badly burnt that Carmen couldn't hug him to comfort him, she could only squeeze his big toe. He was being fed through a tube. Most of his left hand was amputated and the fingers on his right hand removed to the first knuckle. He had nerve damage in his right leg, inhalation burns in his lungs and diminished eyesight.

'I started fighting every day to recover, pushing through the pain and the limits that I was being told defined me. My days were filled with a gruelling regimen of surgeries, skin grafts and physical therapy, but I refused to quit. My attitude was simple: stay positive and never, ever quit. When your life changes as dramatically as mine, there's a chance you might give up. I never let that happen to me and I never will. Everyone knows if you quit before you start, you're done. I will never let the guy who set that bomb get the satisfaction that they ruined my life.'

When he'd first come round from his coma, the doctors had told DT four things. First, he had at best a 15 per cent chance of survival. Second, even if he did live then he'd be on a permanent respirator for the rest of his life. Third, he'd be in hospital for at least the next 18 months. And finally, he'd never walk again.

Six weeks after being told all this, DT walked out of the hospital. No respirator.

In 2010, he became the first 100 per cent disabled airman to re-enlist in the USAF. Now he was at the Invictus Games, with the official rank of Technical Sergeant and the unofficial but no less accurate one of Maximum Badass. 'I am like the legendary phoenix,' he said. 'I am reborn from these ashes and these flames have made me stronger.' Whenever he went to the powerlifting bench for another attempt, he wore his lucky hat, the one he was wearing at the time of the IED blast. That may not have been most people's idea of 'lucky', but it was DT's. Who knows what would have happened if he hadn't been wearing it? Lucky hat didn't cover it; 'Invictus Hat' was more like it.

In his opening speech, Prince Harry had promised that lives would be changed over the weekend. By the time Sunday and the closing concert came round, that was exactly what had happened. Every one of the 400-plus competitors had had their own Invictus moment, no matter their nationality, their sport, their gender or their placing. They'd all had the simple triumph of saying – more, of *knowing* – a fundamental truth: 'I beat this and I am better for it.'

Harry had made his opening speech in a suit and tie. Now he was dressed in jeans and a fleece. It was a time for celebration rather than formality. The Foo Fighters were waiting in the wings for their gig to start, but first the Prince had a few words to say.

'What a phenomenal few days! These Games have shone a spotlight on the unconquerable character of servicemen and women and their families – their Invictus spirit. These Games have been about seeing guys sprinting for the finish line and then turning round to clap the last man in. They have been about teammates choosing to cross the line together; not wanting to come second, but not wanting the other guys to either. These Games have shown the very best of the human spirit.

'We knew these Games would inspire people to overcome their challenges, whether mental or physical, and try something they thought impossible. A lady called Kara emailed us about what the Games have meant to her. She said: "I have struggled for 10 years with auto-immune problems, but now I feel like I can start seeing myself as someone new. Up until my awareness of the Invictus Games, I was living in memories and mourning for what I had lost when I got sick at 24. In my mind, my life was over and I was just waiting to be done, because I was not capable of doing or living like I used to. I'm starting to think now that my game has just begun too."'

As the Foo Fighters came on and the competitors danced with new friends who they felt they'd known for a lifetime, Stephan Moreau caught up with Jonas Hjorth Andersen, one of the Danes he'd been riding with in the road race before his crash. Jonas was still wearing the silver medal he'd won that day, and happily posed for a selfie with Stephan. Only later, when Stephan was back home in Canada and looking through the photos of a week he'd never forget, did he see that Jonas had been pushing the medal towards him while their picture was being taken.

And it wasn't surprising that Jonas of all people should have so embodied the Invictus spirit. Six years before, while serving in Afghanistan, he had helped load the coffin of one of his friends onto a British military plane leaving Kandahar Airfield. The young man who had been killed, the one whom everyone had liked, had been Morten Krogh Jensen, and the plane had been the one taking Prince Harry home in a hurry – the very flight, in fact, which had given Harry the first germ of the idea which would change not just his life but those of hundreds of others too.

KAI CZIESLA, GERMANY

Kai Cziesla had always been an adventurer. Before the Army he'd been a policeman and a firefighter. As far as he was concerned, the more action the better, so when he was posted to Afghanistan he was thrilled.

He'd been there three and a half months when his armoured vehicle was hit by an IED while on patrol in Kundus. He was lucky not to lose his right leg, though at times in the year of various surgeries which followed he didn't feel so lucky. When he closed his eyes he found himself back in the armoured vehicle, the blast going off and his leg shattered beneath him.

Not that some people had much sympathy. There is probably no country in Europe whose people have such conflicted attitudes towards their armed forces as Germany does. The memory of Nazism, 12 short but seismic years, hangs over the nation's psyche to this day, and the German Army is one of the most visible targets of that confusion. In some cities, soldiers don't go out on the streets in uniform. In America, those soldiers would be applauded and thanked for their service. In Germany, they might be spat at or even attacked.

Kai tried to return to active service, but his leg injury meant he couldn't operate at full capacity. Besides, it seemed to discomfit his colleagues. Some of them chose to ignore it and made no concessions, others paid it too much attention. Kai just wanted to be normal again, but normality – at least as defined in Army terms – was gone.

Fifteen months after his injury, he joined a three-week pilot course for disabled people at the sports school in Warendorf. They helped him work on what he could achieve rather than what he couldn't. He set himself personal goals rather than strictly military ones – 'For the first time, I could take my daughter to her bed in the evening from the living room. It was indescribable, a real success.'

Kai took up indoor rowing and soon became so adept at it that he ended up not just competing, but coaching the rest of the German team too. In Orlando, he won silver in the four-minute category. That medal, and the date of his injury, are now immortalised in tattoo on his injured leg.

8

THE MASTER
OF MY FATE

The first Invictus Games had always been intended to be just that: the first in a series, not a one-off. Their success meant that the search for another city to take up the mantle was quickly under way. 'It was an event that captured hearts, challenged minds and changed lives,' said Prince Harry in July 2015 on the official announcement of the Orlando Games. 'But for every competitor at the first Invictus Games, there are hundreds of others who would benefit from having the same opportunity.'

In November 2014, two months after the London Games had closed, the bidding process 'for the next Invictus Games in spring 2016 and summer 2017' opened. The timescale was interesting on two fronts. First, it reflected the acceptance that there was not enough time left for any city to host a Games in 2015. Yes, London had managed it inside a year, but that had been down to exceptional circumstances – in particular, the nucleus of an experienced organising committee already in place and the unique qualities of public relations and access which came with being Prince Harry. Second, the stipulation of 'spring' implied a warm-weather venue, or at least a venue where the weather was warmer than London (which the cynic would have suggested did not rule out that many places).

So it was with great pleasure that, in July 2015, Prince Harry announced that Orlando would host the second Games in 10 months' time: May 2016. Orlando was a natural choice: good weather and a ready-made venue at the ESPN Wide World of Sports complex within Disney World. What better place for friends and family to come and support? There was also a strong military connection to the area: the Orlando VA Medical Center serves over 90,000 veterans.

London 2014 had enjoyed support at the highest level, and it was clear that Orlando 2016 would benefit from similar. Former President George W. Bush would host a policy symposium during the Games in order to discuss ways for veterans to receive appropriate care and reduce the stigma attached to 'the invisible wounds of war' such as PTSD, traumatic brain injury and other psychological health issues.

'Invictus 2014 smashed stigma on visible injuries,' said Harry at the symposium. 'This can do the same on invisible injuries.' It was a theme which he would also emphasise in his speech at the opening ceremony.

And the Obamas, who had succeeded George W. Bush and his wife, Laura, in the White House, were bringing their own star quality to proceedings. When Harry went to Washington in late 2015, Michelle Obama introduced him to the crowd at a basketball match with the words: 'All right, ladies, Prince Harry is here. Don't act like you didn't notice.'

A week or two before the Games, the President and the First Lady sent Harry a threatening but tongue-in-cheek video message. With three uniformed service personnel in the background, Michelle said, 'Hey, Prince Harry. Remember when you told us to bring it at the Invictus Games?' Pointing at the camera, President Obama added, 'Careful what you wish for', while the service personnel made scary faces and mimed a 'boom' microphone drop.

'I spent maybe a week thinking "How the hell am I going to top this?"' said Harry, according to a report in the *Mirror*. 'I just thought to myself, there's only one thing I can do. I'm going to have to ring the Queen. And I think it was almost as though you could see that look in her face, at the age of 90, thinking, "Why the hell does nobody ask me to do these things more often?"'

By way of reply, they filmed the Queen watching the Obamas' message on Harry's mobile and saying witheringly,

'Oh really. *Please*,' while Harry dropped his own imaginary microphone and sent a 'boom' back across the Atlantic.

'We did one take from two angles,' the *Mirror* recorded Harry as saying at the time. 'She's the Queen, she's busy! You don't have more than 90 seconds to get that right. We didn't practise, it was just one take. Also, she's so incredibly skilled, she only needs one take. Meanwhile, I was like a gibbering wreck. I was more nervous than anyone else. It was great fun and I hope everyone enjoyed it.'

Great fun indeed, and more importantly good publicity for the Games themselves.

When Harry opened London 2014, it had been a step into the unknown. Opening Orlando 2016 felt different: Invictus was no longer just a Games, it was a movement, a groundswell, a manifestation of Victor Hugo's famous statement that 'There is nothing so powerful as an idea whose time has come'.

There was no Brigade tie this time, and the suit was a little more casual. 'I'm a long way from London tonight,' Harry began. 'But when I look out and I see so many familiar faces, servicemen and women, their friends and their families and all the people who have got them here, I feel like I'm at home.

'I joined the Army because for a long time I just wanted to be one of the guys. But what I learned through serving was that the extraordinary privileges of being a prince gave me an extraordinary opportunity to help my military family. That's why I had to create the Invictus Games – to build a platform for all those who have served to prove to the world what they have to offer.

'Over the next four days you will see things that in years past just wouldn't have been possible. You will see people who by rights should have died on the battlefield – but instead they are going for gold on the track or in the pool. You will be inspired, you will be moved, and I promise you will be entertained.

'While I have your attention, though, I want to briefly speak about an issue that for far too many of you is shrouded in shame and fear. An issue that is just as important for many of you watching at home as it is for those of you in this stadium tonight. It is not just physical injuries that our Invictus competitors have overcome, every single one of them will have confronted tremendous emotional and mental challenges.

'When we give a standing ovation to the competitor with the missing limbs, let's also cheer our hearts out for the man who overcame anxiety so severe he couldn't leave his house. Let's cheer for the woman who fought through post-traumatic stress and let's celebrate the soldier who was brave enough to get help for his depression.

'Over the next four days you will get to know these amazing competitors. They weren't too tough to admit that they
struggled with their mental health, and they weren't too
tough to get the help they needed. To those of you watching
at home and who are suffering from mental illness in silence
– whether a veteran or a civilian, a mum or a dad, a teenager
or a grandparent – I hope you see the bravery of our Invictus
champions who have confronted invisible injuries, and I
hope you are inspired to ask for the help that you need.

'To end, can I just say thank you to all of you guys. You
are fierce competitors. You are role models that any parent
would be proud to have their children follow. You've made
me a better person. You are about to inspire the world and
I'm proud to call you my friends. So let's put on a hell of a
show in memory of all of our fallen comrades who didn't
make it back. We are Invictus!'

The second Invictus Games were open.

For Sarah Rudder, one of the high points of that opening
ceremony had been seeing the Marine Corps Silent Drill
Team doing their routine. It was what had made her want to
be a Marine when she'd first seen it, aged 12, and two
decades later, it had lost none of its thrill.

For her, the Orlando Games were 'a lifesaver in so many
ways'. It was the first time she'd been in a crowd for 15
years, and yet she was OK – not totally relaxed about it,

sure, but with enough coping mechanisms now in place to ensure that she could deal with it. A few years before, when she hadn't been able to deal with fireworks, even the sound of the starting gun would have been too much for her. But now she could just clear her mind when competing – 'I didn't think about anything, just went as hard as I could when the gun went.'

'As hard as I could' proved plenty hard enough. Sarah won the very first medal of the Orlando Games and scarcely let up after that. By the end she had seven medals in all: gold in lightweight powerlifting, one-minute indoor rowing, discus and the 100m, and silver in the shot-put, four-minute indoor rowing and the 200m. In the last of those, the 200m, she fell near the end after her prosthetic leg, the one with 'Wonder Woman' on it, gave way – 'My leg didn't want to keep up with me' – but she got up, crossed the line and fell again into the embrace of her conqueror, Marion Blot from France. The crowd gave them both a standing ovation.

Bart Couprie competed in four sports: indoor rowing, wheelchair rugby, wheelchair basketball and swimming. He didn't win one medal, let alone seven, but he loved every minute of the Games nonetheless – 'I'd watched the London Games and followed friends' results online. When I saw the Foo Fighters at the final concert I thought, "Oh, you bastards", because they're my favourite band and it would have been awesome to be there. But then I figured maybe it was just as well that I wasn't, because to be there something pretty shit has to happen to you in the first place. Be careful what you wish for, eh?'

It was only a couple of months later that he was diagnosed with cancer, and even once Orlando was announced as host city for 2016, it still didn't really register on his radar – 'I had a full complement of limbs, so I didn't think I was eligible.' Even when he'd been put straight and was heading for his first training camp, he was finding it hard to shake off the feeling that cancer somehow wasn't sufficiently serious to qualify for Invictus – which in itself felt a little absurd, given the impact it was having on pretty much every other aspect of his life. The camp knocked any such doubts clean out of the window – 'I started off thinking, "Am I sick enough to be here?" By the end of the camp the only question was, "Am I good enough to be here?"'

From across the Tasman Sea, Darlene Brown was also loving her first Invictus Games. 'God, it was so much fun – it was the most exciting thing I'd ever done in my entire life! For the powerlifting, we came out one by one through a smoke machine with the crowd screaming. It was like being in a movie.' She had only taken up powerlifting a few months before, and during her very first session a TV crew had come into the gym and started to film – 'The reporter

227

asked me what my personal best was. I could hardly lift the 20kg bar, but I couldn't tell them that – and out of nowhere I had this brainwave and said, "Oh, that's a secret", like I was some hotshot who didn't want her competitors to know anything!'

From struggling to lift 20kg, Darlene now lifted double that to win silver (behind, inevitably, Sarah 'Wonder Woman' Rudder). It was Australia's first medal of the Games. 'I never thought I could do anything like that. It was – it was just amazing. The whole thing was. Only when I went to Orlando did I realise how much I'd been grieving for the whole military lifestyle, for the mateship and camaraderie. And Prince Harry! I was starstruck, like a stupid teenager, when he appeared. I threw my husband out of the way to get to him!'

For Sarah, Bart and Darlene, their first time at the Invictus Games had proved as rewarding as they'd hoped. For those who'd competed in London and were now back for another go, Orlando was no less special. 'I really trained hard for this one,' Josh Boggi said. 'Two months in Mallorca, no distractions, total focus. "Let's have this properly," I thought.' In London he'd won bronze and come fourth in his two cycling events. Here, he won silver in both. Franck Robin of France won gold in both disciplines, as he had in London, but the gaps were much closer this time round: four seconds in the time trial and only half a second in the road race. On a whim,

Josh entered the indoor rowing later that day – no point letting all that arm strength and cardio training go to waste – and won gold in both the four-minute and one-minute races.

It wasn't just the improvement in his own performances which pleased him, or even the effect that improvement and the training necessary for it were having on the rest of his life; it was the way Invictus forced you and those around you to reassess things. On the bus to the venue one morning, Josh found himself sitting next to Bart Couprie. They'd never met before, but started chatting. He told Bart how he'd been injured, Bart told him about his cancer. Josh sympathised and said he couldn't even imagine how Bart was dealing with it.

For a moment, Bart was nonplussed. Here was a guy with one arm and no legs saying he couldn't imagine how to deal with cancer. Was he taking the piss? Was this some obscure trope of British humour? No, Josh was being quite serious. He explained that he knew exactly what he was dealing with every day: his limbs weren't going to grow back, nor were they going to get worse. Bart's condition, on the other hand, was still fluctuating.

Besides, everybody – members of the public, that was – could see what had happened to Josh, and so they made allowances for it. Bart's ailments weren't nearly so obvious.

If you didn't know about the chemo and the injections, you'd just assume he was a balding bloke with man boobs, and there was no shortage of those around. Bart got off that bus more enlightened than he'd been when he'd boarded it.

There were other connections, too. Bart had never met Stephan Moreau either, but when they competed in the indoor rowing they were practically inseparable in the results table. In the four-minute race, Stephan was one place and eight metres ahead of Bart; in the one-minute race, Bart was one place and a single metre ahead of Stephan. The margins were narrow and totally unimportant in the wider scheme of things; the connections were priceless.

'Orlando pretty much saved my life,' Stephan said. 'London had been great, but after that I went through a really bad patch. My wife and I separated. I fell off my bike and had concussion. Physically and emotionally, I was broken. Then Orlando was announced and I knew I had something to train towards again. That pulled me round. When I got there, I went to see as many events as possible, to soak it all up. Only at the end did I realise that I still had three days unused on my four-day Disney pass! I'd been too engrossed in the Games to give Mickey Mouse a thought.'

For Mike Goody, it was business as usual: four gold medals in London, and now four more in Orlando. His opponents would surely be sick of the sight of him were he not such a palpably decent bloke.

Mary Wilson and Maurillia Simpson didn't compete in Orlando, though Simi was there as part of the Invictus Games Choir which sang at the opening ceremony. The choir was conducted by Gareth Malone, who had done such amazing work with the military wives of Chivenor, five years before. On the first day of the Games, still on a high from the reception the choir had received the night before, Gareth said: 'It's had a profound effect on me. I'm going to reassess my own life. That sounds really grand, but you come here and it's the word I've heard so many times before, humbling, but I can't think of another word. You just feel like, I am so lucky, and these people are so amazing, I must do more.' He'd conducted choirs on much bigger stages, but few – if any – had been as special and significant as this one. 'I'm pretty overwhelmed.'

The Invictus Games family was growing and its members were writing their own pages in its history: none more so perhaps than Elizabeth Marks.

Elizabeth joined the US Army aged 17 as a combat medic. Two years later in Iraq, she was badly injured in circumstances she has always refused to discuss. Her left leg is now encased in an IDEO (intrepid dynamic exoskeletal orthosis), and most of her right leg is covered in a giant tattoo.

There's a rather beautiful country and western song by the band Montgomery Gentry called 'Tattoos and Scars'. It recounts the story of two men, one young and one old, who get chatting in a bar. The young guy, cocky and boastful, talks the old man through the tattoos he's got: one from Memphis in 'some back old alley dump', another from Dallas when he 'sure was good and drunk'. Then it's the old man's turn. He shows his 'ragged old and jagged ordinary scars' – one from Paris in a war long before the young guy was born, another 'when I was half your age, workin' on my daddy's farm'.

The message is clear. Tattoos are ornaments, scars are earned. 'Tattoos and scars are different things.'

And normally they are. But not for someone like Elizabeth. Her tattoo sits on her scars, which made the inking process much more painful than usual. And if you know how to read her tattoo, you know how to read her story. There's a crow, battered and bruised but still alive: that's her. On the crow's ankle bracelet there's a red cross – pretty much the only splash of colour in the entire tattoo – which represents being a combat medic. The dog tags carry the name of her father, James, a Vietnam vet whom she has described as her inspiration.

Unable to continue serving as a combat medic, Elizabeth chose to continue to help her colleagues through swimming. The better she could be, the more she could do in spite of her injuries, the more inspiration she knew she could provide: 'When I step onto the blocks, I never think, "I want to win," I think, "I want to pour all of myself into this race because there are people who can't physically, mentally or emotionally, do that." So it's my way of performing for them. Each time it starts to get painful, I know I have so much support behind me, the solidarity of all my Invictus brothers and sisters and everyone who competes in that realm.'

And if that was hard enough before London 2014, it was nothing compared to what happened there – or rather, what *didn't* happen there. Elizabeth had arrived in London for those Games in good physical shape and favourite for several titles but pretty much from the moment she landed, she felt sick. The doctors kept an eye on her, and when her condition deteriorated, she was taken to hospital, where they found that her lungs were filled with fluid and she couldn't breathe properly.

She was transferred to Papworth Hospital, one of the country's premier heart and lung hospitals (Sir Terence English had performed Britain's first heart transplant there in 1979). At Papworth the doctors put her in a medically induced coma and onto an extracorporeal membrane oxygenation (ECMO), a system which allows oxygen to enter the patient's bloodstream outside the body and is only used in the most serious cases of heart and lung failure.

Elizabeth missed the London Games altogether. She has recovered, but not totally. With her lungs less efficient than they were before, she goes into such oxygen debt when she swims that she goes temporarily blind and needs her coach to tap her with a pad on the end of a stick a couple of strokes out from the end of every length so she knows when to turn.

But swim she does, and extraordinary well too. In Orlando she won four gold medals in the ISB category: the 50m backstroke, 50m breaststroke, 50m freestyle and 100m freestyle. The last one she was particularly proud of: the extra distance was so hard for her that when she touched the wall she didn't know she'd won and was only vaguely aware of where she was.

It was a few minutes before she was sufficiently *compos mentis* to stand on the podium for her gold medal. Prince Harry himself presented it to her. She stood proud with hand over heart during the anthems, posed for photos with the two British competitors who'd won silver and bronze, and then caught up with Harry as he was on his way to the next event.

She took the gold medal off and handed it back to him. 'Would you do something for me?' she asked. 'Take this back to England and give it to the team at Papworth who saved my life.' It wasn't much, but then again nothing would be enough to repay what she owed them. She just wanted them to know that she'd been thinking of them, and that it was only because they'd helped her that she could continue doing her best to help others. That was why she'd wanted them to have the medal she'd found toughest to win: because it had hurt the most, it had hurt so much, but it hurt in the best possible way because she was still alive.

Elizabeth's gesture wasn't the only one which caught the public's imagination. There was also Australia's Mark Urquhart, who had been left paraplegic following two parachute accidents and had chosen to have his legs amputated in order to honour a promise he'd made to his daughter – that the day she got married he'd walk her down the aisle.

In Orlando he dominated the IT5 wheelchair races. He'd won the 100 metres, 200 metres and 400 metres, and now he was going for the clean sweep in the 1500 metres. But near the end he could see that his rival, Steve Simmons of the US, was struggling. 'It was extremely hot and his poor old arms couldn't cope with the last lap of the oval,' said Mark. 'As a fellow soldier I just reached out and helped him. He came up beside me and he wanted to go hand in hand over the line. I said, "Yeah, mate, no worries" and then I grabbed the back of his chair and pushed him along in front of me so he got the gold.'

And as always with the Invictus Games, those who came last were appreciated just as much as those who came first.

It took Kelly Elmlinger of the USA 20.61 seconds to win the Women's IT4/IT5 100 metres; it took Ulfat Al-Zwiri of Jordan more than two minutes to complete. But Ulfat, who had been severely injured in a car crash while on duty, received a standing ovation from both the crowd and her fellow competitors as she made her agonisingly slow but fully determined way down the track, and when she finally made it over the line it was the seven women who'd beaten her – four British and three American – who were first to embrace her.

In the stands, her parents, Yasin and Basema, waved the Jordanian flag and choked back the tears. 'We are very happy and very proud of Ulfat for what she has done today for herself and for her country at the Invictus Games,' her father said. 'It has been wonderful to see how far she has come in her recovery to be able to participate in a major international event like this. She has represented her country and herself very well.'

His sentiments were echoed by Prince Mired Raad Zeid Al-Hussein, chairman of the Board of the Hashemite Commission for Disabled Soldiers in Jordan. 'We hope that Ulfat's performance and example at the Invictus Games will help to shatter stereotypes about what is possible for injured soldiers to achieve in Jordan and elsewhere. We also hope that Ulfat will be a role model for young girls in Jordan about what they can do through sport and in society.'

For the Invictus Games are about all the nations which compete, not just the larger ones. It had taken the Afghanistan team almost 24 hours to reach Orlando, and through no fault of their own they had come ill-equipped: no coaches, a team manager none of them had met before, no prosthetic limbs, scarcely a tracksuit of their own. They had had neither the funds nor the facilities to train properly; even the main Afghan training base in Kabul had no rowing machine.

So the other teams helped them out. The Americans covered the cost of the Afghanis' flights, hotels and food. During the powerlifting, the Australian lifters spotted for their Afghan competitors and encouraged them. When Afghanistan briefly took the lead against France during the sitting volleyball match between the two nations, the crowd roared as loud as at any time during the Games.

And from the all too visible evidence of disparity – state-of-the-art prosthetic legs for the Westerners, 25-year-old hooks for the Afghanis – may yet come some good. Will Reynolds, the US team captain who lost part of his left leg in a Baghdad bomb, said: 'I've got eight (artificial) legs – more than I need. Some of the legs I can't even wear. And to know there are other service members out there wearing stuff that's not serviceable is unacceptable.' He suggested a donation programme in which discarded prosthetics are sent to countries like Afghanistan, which desperately need them.

The Georgians were also enjoying their time in Orlando. Always good value at international sporting events, as countless players and fans will testify from the last four Rugby World Cups, they play hard, on and off the field, and it's a brave or foolish man who takes on a Georgian in a drinking match. They were good value here too. When Giorgi Bochorishvili won silver in the men's IT6 100 metres, the cheers from his teammates could be heard from all around the stadium.

'For the first moment I could not realise what happened,' Giorgi said. 'When I understood, it was an amazing feeling to bring a medal back home.'

And they lit up the sitting volleyball tournament with their formation chanting and intense team huddles. They ran the British close in the semi-final – the two teams had been sharing tips via Skype in the run-up to the Games – and then defeated the Netherlands to win the bronze medal. 'The Games have been amazing,' said Besarion Gudushauri, Georgia's captain. 'It's allowed us to make friendships, restart our sporting careers and encourage others to achieve by joining us. I am humbled to be a part of these Games.'

Him, and everyone else.

RAHMON ZONDERVAN, NETHERLANDS

The national flag on the coffin was what Rahmon Zondervan remembered most. Rahmon was eight years old, and his grandfather had just died. He remembered the red, white and blue draped perfectly across the lid. His grandfather had been a soldier, and Rahmon wanted to be one too. He watched war movies and fell in love with the idea of army life.

He joined up at 17, and was deployed to Afghanistan pretty much immediately after basic training. Three months into his tour, he was wounded by a suicide-controlled IED in Uruzgan province which killed the man – a colleague, a friend – standing next to him. Rahmon lost his right eye, badly damaged his eardrums and wrist, and needed more than 200 stitches on his arms, legs and face – 'In the two and a half years after the attack I underwent 13 operations, ranging from work on my eye to removing pieces of boxer shorts which the blast had driven into my body.'

He continued in the Infantry during his rehabilitation, but like many others in similar situations found himself caught between two stools: he obviously couldn't go back out on combat missions, but still felt himself to be a soldier with much to offer the Army. In the end, he left the Infantry to retrain as an army physiotherapist. He'd always been a keen sportsman and had run a lot during his rehab to keep fit and relieve his stress and anxiety, so the move made sense in more ways than one.

The physio course was a civilian one, so Rahmon spoke with his new classmates about what had happened to him – 'That's one advantage of my type of injuries: they're very visible, so people do ask you about them.' He worked hard to get his diploma as quickly as possible. 'I had it much easier than some of my classmates, who needed part-time jobs or loans to do the course. The Army was paying for me to do it all, so I was very grateful.'

He captained the Dutch team in London – 'a big honour' – and went to Orlando too, both times with the Invictus Games 'I AM' logo painted on his prosthetic eye. 'They were so different, the two Games, in lots of ways, but I can't say which one I preferred. I give them both a big fat 10! The camaraderie and the support is unbelievable.'

Like many other competitors, Rahmon is happy to give up his place for Toronto if need be so that someone else can have a go and experience what he has.

'I try to get all I can out of life, every day. The way I see it, if I'm not enjoying life then my buddies died for nothing. I don't put a limit on what I can do. I've found that many people look for the worst: "Oh, I'm missing an eye, I can't do this or that or the other." My advice is to just try it. Even with one eye I can now drive and shoot again. You can do more than you think you can.'

THE CAPTAIN OF MY SOUL

London 2014, Orlando 2016, Toronto 2017, Sydney 2018 ... At the time of writing, that is all we know so far. Where the Invictus Games go after that, and when they go there, is still to be decided. There is no set timetable, no rigid cycle which must be maintained, come hell or high water. The Games will go on for as long as they're needed, whether that's one year or 100 years. The one thing which everyone involved wants to avoid is any sense that the Games may one day be held just because it's always been that way: the Games should go on, and will go on, for as long as they continue to change lives.

The phrase 'life-changing injury' or 'life-changing illness' is almost always a negative one. In that context, the word 'change' implies reduction: reduction of ability, reduction of opportunity, reduction of life quality itself. And this, of course, is often the case – but not always. The Invictus Games have shown that 'life-changing' can mean just that – 'change' scented with overtones of freshness and positivity. The opposite of change is stasis, and stasis leads to stagnation, to withering and to death – a death which pretty much every Invictus competitor has stared in the eye and faced down.

'I'm still here,' says Josh Boggi. 'I'm still the same person as I was before – I've just got a few limbs missing. Yes, I did want to be a soldier, but now I'll settle for just being me.' And if the man who set the IED which almost killed him walked in here now, to this Salisbury coffee shop where we're talking, what would he do? Josh holds up his one remaining hand: 'I'd shake his hand.' Honestly? 'Honestly. He was doing his job, I was doing mine. It wasn't personal.'

Sarah Rudder looked round the stadium in Orlando at her fellow competitors: men, women, amputees, post-traumatic stress survivors, cancer sufferers and more. They were all wearing the colours of the nations they were so proud to represent, but those flags united more than they divided them – 'We fought the same war together. We suffered together, we got injured, we died together. And we survived together. I lost 13 years trying to save that darn leg. Now I'm going to get those years back.'

For Stephan Moreau, it's simple: 'Something really significant happened to me with Invictus. I'm not the same person any longer.' Maurillia Simpson found similar: 'It's the beginning of a new dream and something I never thought would happen. It never ends there. If you have that breath of life in you there is a purpose, there's always something you can do.'

Mike Goody is helping to raise money for Canine Partners, the company his girlfriend Sara Trott works for, and is also giving motivational talks. 'If I could go back to myself under that vehicle, I'd say it'll be tough, hard, rough, but stay strong and life will get better. The future's wide open for whatever you want it to be. You might have to do some things differently, but you will do them.'

Near the end of our Skype chat, Darlene Brown suddenly laughs. 'You know, a year ago, I could never have done this interview – I'd have been a bawling mess. Invictus has made me think anything's possible. I've learned to ask for help and look after myself more. I'm happy not to be angry. It was like someone has moved into my head, and now they're gone again. And for post-traumatic sufferers, we can't go to the Paralympics, so Invictus is our place, you know? Who knew the world was so full of nice people?' She laughs again. 'Mind you, my illness did have its positives. Since I never went out, I ended up paying off the mortgage in record time!'

Bart Couprie should, with any luck, have his final injection and be in full remission from prostate cancer in late 2017: 'Cancer has taken so much from me, but it's also given me so much. Without cancer I'd never have gone to Invictus, never met presidents nor princes, never met all these incredible people – guys who've won the Medal of Honor, the VC, those guys. Those memories will last so much longer than any embarrassment I had about my illness. When life flips you the bird, flip it the bird back. Scar tissue is stronger than skin.'

For Mary Wilson, the Invictus Games were most of all her fellow competitors and teammates – 'They're a core of people I'd do anything for. My life is so much better for having met them.' And that includes Prince Harry: 'I told him, "Your mum would be proud of you," and she would be. She would be very proud.'

Harry is still a young man with decades ahead of him, but he will surely be hard-pressed to find any cause whose impact matches what he has already achieved with the Invictus Games. I spoke to dozens of people while writing this book, and not a single one of them had a bad word to say about him. The more people who told me of their encounters with him, the more I was reminded of Raymond Chandler's instruction in the November 1945 edition of the *Atlantic Monthly* that 'down these mean streets a man must go who is not himself mean, who is neither tarnished nor afraid. He must be a complete man and a common man and yet an unusual man. He must be, to use a rather weathered phrase, a man of honor, by instinct, by inevitability, without thought of it, and certainly without saying it … The story is this man's adventure in search of a hidden truth, and it would be no adventure if it did not happen to a man fit for adventure. If there were enough like him the world would be a very safe place to live in without becoming too dull to be worth living in.'

The Invictus Games are at once quintessentially Harry's and yet set totally apart from him. They are not an end in themselves, but a springboard to things wider, deeper and greater. Ken Fisher, Chairman of Invictus Games Orlando 2016, spoke of his three aims: honouring the service these men and women have given and the sacrifices they have made, educating people around the world about the impact of injuries, visible and invisible, and inspiring others who may feel themselves lost to re-engage with society, rebuild their spirit and restore their self-esteem.

The men and women of the Invictus Games could do amazing things for our society, if only we let them. In his closing speech at London 2014, Prince Harry said, 'By definition, servicemen and women are highly skilled, well trained and motivated people. Many of those injured are young men and women with their whole lives ahead of them. For those no longer able to serve in the Armed Forces, the future is often uncertain. We should be there ready to support them, if or when they need it. For a few this may mean long-term physical and mental support, but for the majority, this means fulfilling employment. Not special treatment, but to be treated as they were before injury, with respect, admiration and recognition of their considerable talent.'

And just imagine what that talent could do. Imagine an Invictus Games competitor come to talk to a school, for example. Imagine the sparks which that talk could fan in a child listening to those stories. Imagine those same stories being told to a youth group, or in a prison, or even an ordinary office environment. We bemoan the slickness and emptiness of our politicians, but here we have a group which actually has something to teach us if only we will listen.

Harry's final remarks at Orlando 2016 were addressed to the competitors, but they apply to all of us, for the Invictus spirit is there for anyone who chooses to take it.

'You are all Invictus. You are now ambassadors for the spirit of these games. Spread the word. Never stop fighting. And do all you can to lift up everyone around you.'